T0277698

JUST ADD
WATER

SARAH HENSHAW

JUST ADD WATER

OVER 100 WAYS TO RECHARGE AND RELAX ON THE UK'S RIVERS, LAKES AND CANALS

ADLARD COLES

LONDON · OXFORD · NEW YORK · NEW DELHI · SYDNEY

ADLARD COLES
Bloomsbury Publishing Plc
50 Bedford Square, London, WC1B 3DP, UK
29 Earlsfort Terrace, Dublin 2, Ireland

BLOOMSBURY, ADLARD COLES and the
Adlard Coles logo are trademarks of
Bloomsbury Publishing Plc

First published in Great Britain 2023

Copyright © Sarah Henshaw, 2023
Illustrations © Louise Turpin, 2023

Sarah Henshaw has asserted her right
under the Copyright, Designs and Patents
Act, 1988, to be identified as Author of
this work

For legal purposes the Endnotes on
p215, Picture credits on p223 and
Acknowledgements on p224 constitute
an extension of this copyright page

All rights reserved. No part of this
publication may be reproduced or
transmitted in any form or by any means,
electronic or mechanical, including
photocopying, recording, or any
information storage or retrieval system,
without prior permission in writing from
the publishers

Bloomsbury Publishing Plc does not have
any control over, or responsibility for, any
third-party websites referred to or in this
book. All internet addresses given in this
book were correct at the time of going to
press. The author and publisher regret any
inconvenience caused if addresses have
changed or sites have ceased to exist, but can
accept no responsibility for any such changes

A catalogue record for this book is available
from the British Library

Library of Congress Cataloguing-in-
Publication data has been applied for

ISBN: PB: 978-1-3994-0045-9;
ePub: 978-1-3994-0046-6;
ePDF: 978-1-3994-0044-2

10 9 8 7 6 5 4 3 2 1

Design by Louise Turpin
Typeset in Frutiger by louiseturpinde ign.co.uk
Printed and bound in India by Replika Press

MIX
Paper from
responsible sources
FSC® C016779
www.fsc.org

To find out more about our authors and
books visit www.bloomsbury.com and sign up
for our newsletters

Every effort has been made to contact the
copyright holders of material reproduced
in this book. If any errors or omissions
have inadvertently been made, they will be
rectified in future editions provided that
written notification is sent to the publishers.

CONTENTS

INTRODUCTION

I am writing this on the first day of spring. In our house, the start of the season is not so much the equinox or improving weather, budding daffodils or any other traditional marker, but simply the first time our son declares his intention to get the paddling pool out of the shed, which was today.

So it's spring, and he'll be in the pool (or prattling on about how he wants to be in the pool) near enough every day now until summer ends, when his interest in water narrows to puddles instead, which is when autumn starts (splashing in them) and then winter (cracking the ice on them).

This is how I've come to measure out the years since he was born. It's also become a sort of barometer for happiness. I see him at his best when he is strategising water pistol fights from the centre of the pool or setting up a triage system at the side for the hapless ladybirds that fall in off the tree.

And I also see something else – that how he integrates different experiences in the same body of water helps him derive greater pleasure from it. Show an adult the same paddling pool and they will likely be stumped for anything more creative than lolling about in there with tinned alcohol and increasingly angry tan lines.

While babies can demonstrate innate swimming reflexes and kids are still fluent in its fun, as adults we often struggle to commune with water in any meaningful way. And that's a shame, because what centuries of water-based spa culture and contemporary studies into wellbeing show us consistently is that water is good for us.

On our inland waterways there are all sorts of reasons why, from beneficial environmental factors, such as less polluted air, to the way they encourage people to be more physically active – swimming, walking, kayaking etc. And then there's the restorative effect they have psychologically – reducing anxiety, boosting our mood. In 2017 the Canal & River Trust began quantifying these benefits with the publication of its 'Waterways & Wellbeing' report. It found some 95 per cent of the waterway users interviewed as part of a towpath survey agreed the network was 'a good place to relax and de-stress'. No surprise that a year later, in 2018, the Trust officially rebranded as a 'waterways and wellbeing charity', with the tagline 'Making life better by water'.

Sometimes it's not so much what our rivers, lakes and canals can give, but what they take away that helps. Spending time by water is a way of stepping off the treadmill of work/social media/household chores. Marine biologist Wallace J Nichols, author of a book called *Blue Mind: How water makes you happier, more connected*

and better at what you do, suggests the fact we invariably leave our laptops and smartphones at home or on the shore when enjoying the water means we're essentially getting 'bandwidth' back. We can do whatever we want with that, he says.

This book is all about ideas for how to use that bandwidth. Ancient history is a good starting point. For the Greeks, 'taking the waters' was often combined with sports and education, while the Romans saw fit to add the arts, food, leisure, socialising and discussion to their public baths. Over the centuries, water therapy lost this reach. It became medicalised and prescribed, and subsequently shed some of the spontaneity. Crucially, too, it became the preserve of a wealthy few rather than accessible to all.

And so until recently it was relatively easy for us to overlook water as a wellbeing asset. I am as guilty of this as anyone. As a child, most days were spent in the pool or being chased down a yellow waterslide in the garden by a hose. Yet come adulthood, the closest I came to water was the Regent's Canal bridge I crossed on the 390 bus on my way to work every day. If I thought anything of that stretch at all, it was, I suppose, that its brown banality was the perfect foil for the bright lights of the city above that I was much more interested in exploring.

Two years later, close to burning out, I left my job and went travelling. Suddenly, the water became synonymous with pleasure again – with river safaris on rubber rings, rock pools, boat trips to remote islands, snorkelling, jet skis, white-water rafting, and the peerless blues of the Great Barrier Reef. I found new, exciting words to jabber about water and, when I got home, even made a life out of it – first by opening a bookshop on a canal boat, then by moving afloat myself, and finally by joining the editorial team of an inland waterways magazine.

When I later crossed the Channel for a new life in France, the rivers, canals and lakes I encountered there saw me become even more hydro-literate as I found replacement swimming spots, a perfect little reach to lark about on in an inflatable raft, ice creams by the port, blessedly flat towpaths on which to train for marathons, a secret forest stream to dip in when summer starts to boil...

These days I am not alone in making a beeline for the nearest expanse of open water. The Covid-19 pandemic and resulting lockdowns have given Brits a new relationship with the waterways on their doorstep. After the first lockdown, British Canoeing reported an exponential growth in membership, welcoming over 25,000 new paddlers to its community. The Canal & River Trust also noted a huge spike in towpath use, particularly along urban navigations.

Perhaps our mindset changed because we finally had time to actually notice the waterways. Towpaths, lakesides and riverbanks became somewhere to relieve the monotony of four walls during confinement, and dampen anxiety about infection rates and home-schooling and lonely relatives and 'new normals'. Later, they became places to snatch moments with friends and families again. They helped us focus beyond immediate uncertainty and gave new shape to our lives.

You could say that Covid briefly ushered in a new age of spa culture – one in which we went back to the natural world and harnessed our waterways for their therapeutic benefits again, or for the sheer fun of it, or sometimes just to let out the grief.

I'd like to see that continue – for wellness escapes on our rivers, lakes and canals to become part of our day-to-day and not merely a pandemic quirk. And for this new appreciation of what water can do for us to build a symbiotic relationship, so that where we take, we also give back through better conservation efforts.

Perhaps reading this will help you reassess the waterways you live by or visit regularly. You can follow the suggestions literally or let them fuel wild tangents. Chiefly, it's about finding your own ways to enjoy them, your own words to extol why life's simply better by water.

Social spaces: riverbanks and towpaths offer a chance to catch up with friends in the fresh air.

None of the activities that follow are intrinsically dangerous or demand huge risks. However, being in or around water will always call for a certain amount of caution and respect. It's worth reading the points below to remind yourself of some of the hazards and how you can stay safe.

- Obvious dangers either in or around the water are often highlighted by safety information, warning signs and flags, so keep your eyes peeled. As a general rule, stay clear of weirs, locks and sluices, which are often linked with strong currents. And try to stay out of the way of boating traffic, which might struggle to see you if you're in the water.

- Not all hazards are immediately visible. Beware of submerged obstacles such as branches, rubbish and the clichéd shopping trolley. Even harder to spot are currents, even though water may appear to be perfectly still on the surface. These can pose problems for even the strongest swimmers.

- It can often be difficult to judge the depth of water. When it comes to canals, for example, most people assume that you can stand up in them, but this is not always the case. Rivers, lakes, reservoirs and docks are generally much deeper, and colder.

- If you're with kids, keep your eyes on them. Show them how to spot hazards, talk about the dangers of straying too close to the edge and tell them how to react in an emergency. Teaching them to swim will also be a massive help.

- Be prepared for the cold – as much as you can. Even on a summer's day, cold water shock can affect your ability to swim, to look after yourself, or to rescue others.

Keep a close eye on children around any body of water, and talk to them about potential dangers beforehand.

- If you're taking part in a water activity regularly, such as rowing or fishing, consider joining a relevant club. These will offer safety advice tailored specifically to your sport/hobby or stretch of water, as well as pointing out more general waterways hazards.

- They might cut a dash in a swimming pool, but inflatable unicorns, flamingos, pizza slices and any other type of lilo, novelty or otherwise, are less impressive on open water. Understand that they can easily be carried away or blown into deep water and may not keep you afloat.

- Drinking alcohol will impair your ability and judgement in and around water, so be sensible.

- The dreaded Weil's disease – the only waterborne disease most of us have heard of – is thankfully pretty rare. However, if you come into contact with water, it's sensible to take a few precautions. These include covering up any cuts or scratches, washing your hands thoroughly, particularly before food or drink, and taking a shower when you get home. If you develop flu-like symptoms within two weeks, see a doctor and mention that you've been in the water.

- Blooms of blue-green algae can spring up on warm, still water over summer, especially in reservoirs and quiet canals, and sometimes produce toxins. These can cause serious health problems for dogs, and skin and stomach issues for humans. Children are more at risk than adults. If you see a warning sign about it, take it seriously.

- If you do find yourself in an emergency situation and need to call for help, bear in mind that large bodies of water aren't conducive to finding someone easily. 'I'm by a boat/bench/big weeping willow' may not cut it. Instead, consider using the what3words app (what3words.com). It divides the entire world into 3-metre squares, giving each one a unique combination of three words to distinguish it. These are easy to say, simple to share and as accurate as GPS coordinates.

Describe any map of the inland waterways network and you'll probably default to a well-used simile about the arteries of a human body. Just as our circulatory system plays a vital role in keeping us alive, so these blue threads of rivers and canals twisting across the country also support important ecosystems.

Yet according to figures released by the Environment Agency, only 14 per cent of England's rivers are in good ecological health, and every single one fails to meet chemical standards. Considering the tremendous job they do providing habitat for plants and wildlife, a buffer against the impacts of climate change, drinking water and space to unwind and exercise, isn't it time we gave them a helping hand?

Most of the suggestions below are worth considering when you're out and about on the waterways, but there are lots of ways you can take conservation of our lakes, rivers and canals further, whether by making simple lifestyle changes, petitioning MPs or supporting a waterways charity to do the important work on your behalf.

• They say charity begins at home. Well, so does waterways conservation. Remember that whatever you flush down the toilet or sink can impact your local river or lake. Use phosphate-free detergents and soaps, and put fat, grease and oil in the bin rather than down the sink to prevent blockages and overflows. Wet wipes are another no-no for the sewer system. In 2021, environmental charity Thames21 released a laser scan showing the extent to which a mound of them in the riverbed in west London had grown: in the space of six years they had swelled to the size of two tennis courts and measured over a metre tall. In the garden, meanwhile, try to avoid using chemical fertilisers and pesticides, high levels of which are ending up in groundwater and rivers. And don't pour unwanted chemicals, including paints and oils, down the drain.

• 'Own' your local waterway. Find out its name if you don't already know or – better still – give specific stretches a memorable nickname. Near where I live, what I call 'Digger Beach' describes a perennially mucky section of riverbank that's perfect for my four-year-old to lug his construction vehicles to play while I have a dip. Forty minutes down the road, the 'Sausage Lake' is how I still mentally refer to the reservoir we first visited to toast our friend Matthew's birthday with chipolatas on a campfire. They might sound dumb, but fostering a sense of proprietorship will make you more motivated to look after these places. If you want to take this even further, consider signing up for one of the Canal

There are lots of things you can do to look after your local waterway, from taking litter home to alerting navigation authorities to potential problems.

& River Trust's official adoption schemes, committing to simple tasks like regular litter picks or creating a new green space for your whole community to enjoy.

- Report problems to the relevant navigation authority, including pollution, fly-tipping, overflowing bins, invasive weeds and obstacles to navigation, like fallen trees.

- When it comes to litter, always take yours home with you and dispose of any dog mess your pet makes. In addition, why not commit to picking up a quota of litter every time you visit the waterways? The Canal & River Trust has a Plastics Challenge in which you pledge to pick up just one piece of plastic. The charity claims that if we did this every time we visited the waterways, within a year there would be no plastic left. Local groups might organise similar initiatives, or you could simply make it a personal resolution.

- There are lots of excellent charities doing incredible work to look after our canals, rivers and lakes and you'll find a list of some of the main ones in the Useful Websites section at the back of this book. Consider making a donation to support their efforts, or volunteering your time to help.

- Write to your MP on decisions that impact your local rivers and lakes. Signing up for newsletters from waterways charities should alert you when there's relevant legislation going through parliament, waterways issues in the news, or campaigns that might benefit from political backing. Many of these organisations provide letter templates, making the whole process even more straightforward.

- Tempting as it may be to have a go at playing lock-keeper, messing around with waterways infrastructure can have serious consequences, including draining whole stretches of canal. As well as endangering wildlife, refilling it can waste precious navigation authority resources – namely, time that staff could better spend on other work to improve the waterway. Less obvious infrastructure casualties include hump-back bridges. Synonymous with Britain's canal network, they were built for the passage of horse-drawn carts, not for today's speeding motorists, who cause up to £1m of damage to them each year. Slow right down when you next drive over one.

- Invasive non-native species of plants and animals are a growing problem on British waters. According to the Non-native Species Secretariat, over 50 different freshwater species have already been found in our lakes, rivers and other waterways, and the number of new arrivals is increasing rapidly. They can easily hitch-hike on equipment, footwear, clothing and boats and cause serious environmental problems when spread. Try to remember the following advice to avoid inadvertently exacerbating the problem: 1) Check your equipment and clothing for living organisms, paying particular attention to damp or hard-to-inspect areas. 2) Clean and wash all equipment, footwear and clothes thoroughly. If you do come across any organisms, leave them at the water where you found them. 3) Dry all equipment and clothing thoroughly as some species can live for up to two weeks in damp conditions.

- If you own a boat or go boating regularly, there are lots of ways to be greener aboard, from saving water by sharing locks to using biofuels in your tank. Download the Inland Waterways Association's Guide to Greener Boating to find out more ☛ waterways.org.uk/campaigns/green-boating-guide

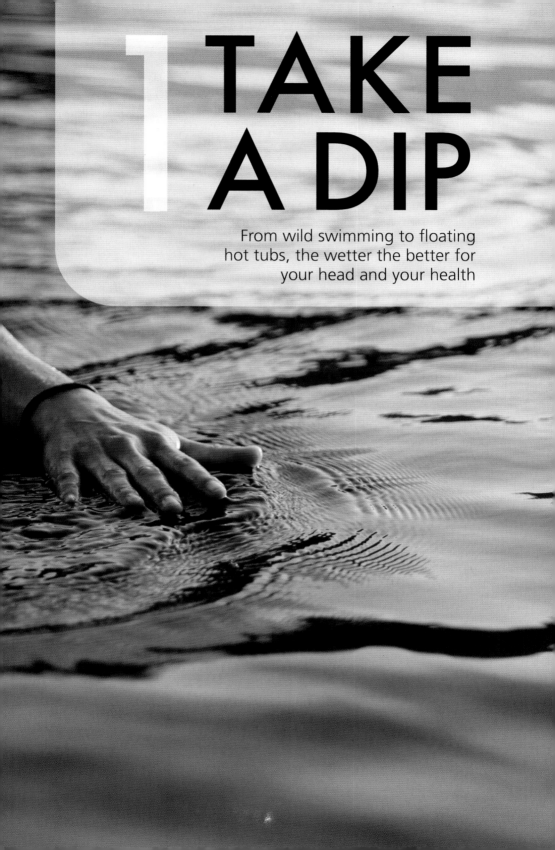

1 TAKE A DIP

From wild swimming to floating
hot tubs, the wetter the better for
your head and your health

Chlorine and floating plasters at the local leisure centre aren't your only options when it comes to taking a dip – our inland waterways can offer a spectacular, and entirely free, alternative to traditional pools.

'Wild swimming' has enjoyed a surge in popularity in recent years, and not just during Bank Holiday heatwave weekends. Instagram feeds are full of bobble hats, swimming cozzies and elated grins well into winter, and converts insist not only is it more fun out of season, it might even be better for you too.

Certainly, in terms of mental health it can have significant benefits. Plunging into cold water regularly has been shown to relieve stress and anxiety. Learning to cope with your body's physical reaction to the temperature is believed to help you react to other stressors less extremely. It also promotes the release of the 'happy hormones' serotonin and dopamine, leading to a post-swim high.

In summer you're likely to stay in the water longer, making it a great way to explore the countryside. You'll experience the thrill of being dive-bombed by dragonflies during your sedate breaststroke, or the simpler pleasure of turning onto your back, picking out a friendly cloud and lazily racing it downriver. Much like a form of mindfulness or meditation, wild swimmers attest it helps them to be in the moment, focusing their mind on how their body feels in the water rather than work worries or other stresses.

It can help people navigate even darker moments too. One of the most beautiful testimonials I've read about wild swimming was by a woman grieving her 20-year-old son. People often talk about the way water feels on your skin, how it invigorates the senses. But for her, full immersion and its associated weightlessness evoked something quite different – an erasing of the body so that, like him, she became almost an absence. It gave her, she said, the connection she craved.

A woolly hat and swimming gloves can make winter dips more palatable.

Getting started

Staying warm both before and after a swim is key to maximising enjoyment, so pile on the layers in winter and try to work up a slight sweat with a brisk walk to the site.

Whether you don a wetsuit or stick with standard swimming wear is entirely your choice. Some people find wetsuits too fiddly to take off afterwards, and enjoy being swaddled by the water itself rather than a layer of neoprene. In any case, the initial cold water 'shock' when you're first submerged is much the same whether you're zipped in or bare-skinned. However, when it's really cold you'll see many wild swimmers in special gloves and socks to protect their extremities.

Getting in is the awful part. Do whatever works for you: splashing water over your limbs first, dithering no deeper than your knees, or grabbing a friend's hand and running in howling. Remember, however, that it will take a few minutes before the cold feeling goes away, so don't turn around and head straight out. Equally encouraging is the fact that the more you do it, the

less you'll feel the cold thanks to your body's clever way of adapting to the temperature. Don't push it, though. It's generally advised not to spend longer than 20 minutes in cold water, and definitely leave sooner if you're shivering.

'Keep your first swim short,' agrees Simon Griffiths, founder of *Outdoor Swimmer* magazine. 'Think of it as a dip rather than a swim. Keep your feet on the bottom to start with and immerse yourself up to your shoulders. The cold may make you gasp initially. Wait until your breathing is calm before trying a few easy strokes. Don't worry about what stroke you use. Just savour the moment and enjoy the experience.'

Once you're out, dry off and layer back up as quickly as you can. It's helpful to organise your clothes so you can put them on fast afterwards – the last thing you want is to be digging around at the bottom of your backpack for ages in just a towel. A thermos of hot sugary tea and a flapjack will also be your friend and help fight what's known among outdoor swimmers as the dreaded 'after drop' – when your core temperature continues to fall even after you've left the water, leading to shivering, feeling faint or even hypothermia.

Where to do it

There are plenty of books offering comprehensive lists of places to take a dip based on geographical location, ability and appetite for being off the beaten track. Online, the Outdoor Swimming Society (outdoorswimmingsociety.com) is an excellent resource and curates numerous platforms where members can find other local bathers or get tips on kit and locations. It also has great advice about keeping on the right side of the law, urging swimmers to make their own judgement and do their homework first about whether it is legal to jump in.

In Scotland there is an explicit (statutory) right to swim or navigate in all water bodies, related to the public Right to Roam. While there is much campaigning in England and Wales for similar rights, these do not yet exist. However, many larger rivers have a statutory public right of navigation created from acts of parliament, which is generally interpreted to extend to swimming. Nevertheless, by-laws may restrict swimming on some stretches (such as near locks) on safety grounds.

Many canals are unsuitable for a dip due to water quality, and generally swimming is not formally permitted on these navigations. The Canal & River Trust, which manages the majority of them in England and Wales, strongly advises anyone interested in open water swimming to make sure they have licensed supervision and support.

For many swimmers, seeking out 'accredited' sites isn't the point. Part of wild swimming's appeal is that frisson of naughtiness that comes from sidestepping authority and claiming the riverbank all for yourself with hastily thrown off clothes and hoots of defiance. Roger Deakin, author of the seminal wild swimming book *Waterlog* and probably the closest thing us Brits have to a patron saint of dipping outdoors, was particularly taken by the idea of secret swimming

spots just waiting to be discovered rather than listed on internet Top Tens or in guidebooks. Word of mouth recommendations from locals, whether they be keen swimmers or not, often spawned some of his most memorable plunges.

Wherever you choose to bathe, do it in company if possible. And not only for your personal safety; the social aspect

of wild swimming is often cited as one of the best things about this sport. If you are going for a solo dip, consider taking an inflatable tow float. You can stow your phone in the centre, sending a GPS tracking signal to a friend or partner to let them know where you are, as well as keys and a whistle. Most floats are luminous too, which makes you more visible in the water should you end up needing help.

Swimming with others is not only more sociable, but safer too.

Sickness from outdoor swimming isn't common, and you can reduce the risks still further by being sensible about where and when you choose to do it.

- If a stretch of water looks inviting, it generally is. If there's scum or a film on the water, or the surface is covered with excessive weed and algae, give it a wide berth. Ditto if there's an off-putting smell.

- If you need a second opinion, take a look at what the wildlife is doing. Healthy water generally attracts fish, plants and birds, so if the pond skaters are haring about on top, the ducks quacking merrily in the middle, and the bankside vegetation looks lush and inviting, you can presume a green light and get right in.

- As a general rule, avoid swimming after heavy rainfall. While most rivers and lakes in the UK are cleaner than they've been for decades, pollution from sewage outfalls, farmland run-off and industrial activity is still a problem. This is often exacerbated by heavy rain, and you're also more likely to encounter storm debris like branches or other hazards that have been washed into the water.

- If you can't help the weather, you can at least make sure you avoid places that are directly downstream of sewage discharges. The Rivers Trust (theriverstrust.org), as part of its campaign for Rivers Fit To Swim In, has an interactive map on its website allowing you to search for these overflows and avoid them.

Hopefully, water companies will start pulling up their socks soon. River clean-ups are springing up across the country and the organisations behind some of these are actively campaigning for bathing water status for their stretches. This means rivers will be under the same rigorous public health testing that coastal waters are subject to, and classified annually as excellent, good, sufficient or poor, based on an assessment of the level of bacteria in the water over the preceding years.

Before plunging in, look for tell-tale signs that the water is clean enough.

PREFER A 'POSH SPLOSH'?

Truly 'wild' swimming isn't for everyone. Some people are nervous of open, unsupervised water, or get squeamish about the feel of mud between their toes or weeds brushing their legs. Others simply prefer safety in numbers and a coffee shop close by rather than complete rural isolation. All of these are understandable, and there are plenty of outdoor swimming solutions for tamer tastes that offer no less of a treat.

Stately swims

I can't be the only one whose default fantasy of an outdoor swim is heavily coloured by *that* lake scene in the 1995 BBC adaptation of *Pride and Prejudice*. While a dripping-shirted Mr Darcy isn't something you'll be able to recreate easily during an al fresco front crawl, you can settle for the breathtaking backdrop of Pemberley (or something similar) by taking a dip within splashing distance of a stately home. A growing number of historic estates now accommodate swims on or near their grounds, and a personal favourite is the view of **Chatsworth House** *(Below)* from the River Derwent in Derbyshire. P&P aficionados will know, of course, that Chatsworth was used for exterior Pemberley scenes in Joe Wright's 2005 film version starring Keira Knightley and Matthew Macfadyen.

Meanwhile, if you've a tolerance for chillier waters, Scotland has a number of popular swim spots beneath spectacular castles and ruins. Try Loch Ness in the Highlands to get up close to Urquhart Castle or, on the west coast, Loch Laich for an eyeful of Castle Stalker.

Chatsworth House on the River Derwent provides a spectacular backdrop for a wild swim.

Hot tubs

It's punnily billed as 'the hottest ticket in town'.
It's certainly the most expensive bath you'll
likely ever have – and the most brazen.
From £33 each, you and up to six people
you know very well can skipper
an electric, self-drive, wood-fired
floating hot tub half-naked
through London's Canary Wharf.
Wearing a branded captain's hat is
an £8 optional extra.

   Skuna Boats (*Right*) operates
from West India Quay, but
the concept is stolen from
Scandinavia's Nordic baths: 1,800
litres of water heated to a toasty 38°C
filling a wooden tub. The boat itself is
powered by a built-in electric motor so
cruising is exceptionally quiet, except for the
good-natured jeers from the quayside bars and
restaurants.

   Cynics might see it as a glorified Instagram opportunity. Or, the waterways
equivalent of the pink stretch limo: something you only do once (preferably not
later than aged 16), and probably never get to live down. But try one out and you
might change your tune and find 75 minutes soaking in deliciously warm water
with a chilled bottle of Prosecco – dare we say it – pleasant? ☛ skunaboats.com

Bathing with the Bloomsbury Set

You'll be jostling with students, locals and literary pilgrims at **Grantchester
Meadows** (*Below*), just south of the city of Cambridge, but boy are you in good
company. This delightful stretch of the River Cam has been a popular swimming

The serene River Cam at Grantchester Meadows.

spot for at least 500 years and counts Lord Byron among its legions of fans over the centuries. In the early 1900s, Virginia Woolf and Rupert Brooke, among others of the Bloomsbury Set, would skinny-dip here, and it is still synonymous with river raucousness.

So much so, in fact, that in summer 2021 King's College Cambridge, which owns Grantchester Meadows, tried to ban swimming here in a bid to stamp out boozy gatherings on the banks. Thankfully, the decision was reversed after a massive public outcry and this gorgeous stretch from Sheep's Green down to the Orchard Tea Gardens in Grantchester is once again open for bathing. Be warned, it can be muddy, but you'll be hard pressed to find a more quintessentially English swimming scene.

If you don't believe me, take Roger Waters' word for it. He penned Pink Floyd's pastoral ballad 'Grantchester Meadows' in praise of the 'laughing' river here, presumably having been introduced to the spot by fellow band member David Gilmour, who lived close to it at the time. Sylvia Plath was similarly drawn to the idyllic environs, and it inspired 'Watercolor of Grantchester Meadows'.

All the luxury of a lido

For the ultimate wellness retreat in a bathing costume, head to Reading's **Thames Lido** (Right). While not on the inland waterways per se, it's so close to the river, and so resplendently luxurious, we're prepared to bend the rules a bit.

'Don't swim on a full stomach' might be standard pool advice, but this is one place where dining out and diving in aren't mutually exclusive. In the same breath that staff tell you today's pool temperature (usually hovering around a pleasant 26°C), you might also be briefed on what time to expect your slap-up two-course breakfast in the adjacent restaurant.

Lidos grew in popularity in the 1930s, when 169 were built across Britain by local councils as recreational facilities. Reading's is exceptional in that it is thought to be the oldest surviving outdoor municipal pool from the Edwardian period. It opened in 1902 as a ladies-only swimming baths, and was initially fed by the Thames.

After it closed in 1974 the pool fell into disrepair and it wasn't until 2013, when Reading Borough Council gave the lido team the green light to work their magic, that painstaking restoration could begin.

Today you feel reassuringly cosseted from the hustle and bustle of 21st-century commuter-ville right outside the lido's doors. There's a holiday vibe, a spa feel, culinary panache and a patchwork of global influences, from the Mediterranean menu to the Scandi-inspired massage rooms. You could believe yourself to be anywhere: Muscat, Manarola, Marrakech or, implausible as it seems, maybe just a stone's throw from Caversham Lock. ☛ thameslido.com

Case study

Stepping into the river, I always feel happy. Immediately any worries or pain are swept away. As I head downstream, grey wagtails, long-tailed tits, bobbing dippers and the occasional kingfisher flash past. I swim all year round, loving the changing seasons. I can smell the wild garlic in early spring, and then watch the May blossom and lush greens of waterside trees engulfing the river. The mandarin ducklings change from cute balls of fluff to gangly chicks running on the water, and then to truculent teenagers lurking at the river's edge. If I'm lucky, a hairy water vole may plop into the water and swim alongside me for a few metres, before scuttling off and squeezing its fat bottom into one of its many holes. There is never a dull swim.

I have swum in the River Derwent in Derbyshire for most of my life. As children we would fish for tiddlers, or wrap ourselves in the green weed and pretend to be water babies. From its origin deep in the Dark Peak, through the magnificent Chatsworth Estate and further south, I have plunged, swum, played and dipped.

Several years ago I discovered the enormous benefits of cold water swimming on my mental health and began to dip most days, all year round. I take a dry bag stuffed with my clothes and towel into the river with me, for as far as I feel like swimming. When I tire or see a spot that takes my fancy, I pop out, unroll my dry bag and get dressed at the riverside.

The chill of the water in winter has helped to keep my acute clinical depression at bay. More recently, I've relied on the river's healing properties to ameliorate the worst symptoms of Long Covid and resultant Chronic Fatigue. Without the Derwent, I'm not sure how I and many close friends would have survived the pandemic; the hysteria, the surging anxiety and the lockdowns. For me, the river is not only stunningly beautiful and home to magnificent flora and fauna, it is my safe place, my haven. ☛ @campbellblackboard

*'I've relied on the river's healing
properties to ameliorate the worst
symptoms of Long Covid'*

2 STRETCH YOUR LEGS

A quick walk with the dog, 100-plus-mile endurance races – and plenty in-between

As someone with a devastatingly poor sense of direction, I've long been seduced by the relative straightforwardness of stomping the towpaths rather than faffing around on fells and moors with a billowing OS map. Add to that a liberal helping of canalside pubs, stunning countryside, wildlife-spotting opportunities, engineering wonders, heritage appeal and a handy lack of stiles to clamber over or livestock to sidestep, and most people will agree our water wanderways have all the ingredients for some fantastic excursions on two legs.

These can range from regular, cursory walks with the dog along a waterway on your doorstep to tackling long-distance paths further afield. Rivers and canals, by virtue of their relative flatness, are also a great way to ease yourself into running or, depending on your level of fitness, test your stamina on an endurance trail. With so much more to see than you would simply pounding the pavements around town, runners often discover they can keep up their pace for longer before fatigue finally sets in.

Exercise is good for you regardless of a waterways setting, of course. Make it a habit and you'll be lowering your risk of heart disease, improving blood pressure and helping to control your weight, among other health perks. Doing it by your local canal or reservoir, however, can be even more beneficial. For a start, in the fresher air you'll avoid gasping in lungfuls of car fumes, and you'll probably feel less self-conscious away from the headlights too. And there are mental health benefits – getting active in the great outdoors has been shown to reduce stress, lower the risk of depression and help with anxiety.

Both walking and running are among the easiest ways to tap into these wellbeing boons. The routes are free to access and you won't have to shell out on fancy equipment to get started. Comfortable shoes and a bottle of water to hand should just about cover all your requirements. And perhaps a fiver stuffed in your pocket for a well-deserved pint at the end.

A few words on walking

Here's the thing: don't feel you have to walk for hours. A brisk 10-minute stroll every day will make a good dent in your recommended 150 minutes of weekly exercise without feeling like a chore. When I say 'brisk', by the way, I mean about 5km (3 miles) an hour, which strictly speaking is faster than a 'stroll' but still convivial enough to carry on a conversation about last night's *Great British Bake Off*, or to exchange pleasantries with a passing boater coming up the lock.

You won't need walking boots – just a pair of old trainers will do – except on muddy stretches or if you're going hell for leather and/or covering a longer stretch. If the latter, take liquid refreshment, snacks, sunscreen and a hat in a small backpack, plus a waterproof jacket if the weather gods aren't smiling on you.

It's difficult to get lost following a canal, river or lake, but it's useful to know some basic local information and get a sense of what's beyond the towpath. There are plenty of apps that will help. Ordnance Survey (ordnancesurvey.co.uk), the national mapping agency, has an obvious and brilliant one, including unlimited use of every OS Explorer and OS Landranger map for the whole of Great Britain if you opt for the premium subscription. You can download them to your phone so you can use them even if you have no signal, and the app works in conjunction with a web version so you can study the routes on a big screen first.

Check out the cheerfully named Go Jauntly app too (gojauntly.com), especially if you're looking for waterway strolls within the confines of a city. In creating walking routes, it gives high priority to both green and blue spaces, aiming to avoid busy roads and high pollution levels. Another good feature in the app is Nature Notes, which works much like a journal to capture the flora and fauna you see while out and about. Its daily prompts are designed to help users take more notice of the natural world around them, and boost wellbeing in the process. In 2018 Go Jauntly also teamed up with the Canal & River Trust to curate some family friendly waterways-specific routes, including along the Kennet & Avon Canal, the River Brent, and Hebden Bridge on the Rochdale Canal.

Remember that linear walks, as most canal and river rambles are, require a bit of logistical dexterity. Traveline (traveline.info) can take the sting out of planning return transport. It's a partnership of transport companies, local authorities and passenger groups sharing routes and times for all travel in Great Britain by bus, rail, coach – and even ferry.

Waterway paths tend to be relatively flat – perfect for people looking to ease themselves into walking or running.

MAKE A WATERWAYS PLOD MORE FUN

Even the most gorgeous stretch of river can sometimes feel like a hard sell when it's competing with a Netflix binge or simply lost the novelty factor. Here are a few ideas to bring new interest to your walks and encourage further exploration.

Hounds of love

Taking your dog or borrowing a friend's is a great way to rediscover the joy of a waterways stroll. Four-legged pals can reduce feelings of loneliness and, as social creatures prone to leaping excitedly upon complete strangers, they're a great ice-breaker if you're looking to make new friends.

Most, but not all, dogs naturally love to get wet in streams and lakes, and for those that are more reluctant there are several ways to encourage them, including choosing stretches of slow-moving water, finding an area that's easy for them to enter and exit, and bringing a buoyant dog toy along for them to retrieve.

Both the Canal & River Trust, which looks after 2,000 miles of waterways in England and Wales, and the National Trust, which cares for over 20 per cent of the Lake District National Park, have recommended routes for pooches on their websites – as well as general advice on canine etiquette. This includes the obvious – pick up any mess – as well as keeping them on a short lead around busy spots like locks and bridges and where there's a danger of disturbing wildlife and livestock. And don't always assume dogs are allowed to leap in. 'However tempting it might be,' CRT's advice continues, 'we can't let dogs swim in the canals. Think of the ducks.'

● *Check that dogs are allowed into the water before letting them off the lead.*

Keep a record

Back in 2017, Scottish Canals launched a so-called Selfie Trail to get more families out exploring the Forth & Clyde Canal between the Falkirk Wheel and the Kelpies, two of Scotland's biggest waterways landmarks. The idea was to show visitors the most interesting photo-stops, buildings and art along the 6.5km (4-mile) route and encourage them to snap and share a selfie on their smartphones along the way. While it might be a bit gimmicky for some, making a record of the things you encounter on your walk is a good exercise in mindful observation. It doesn't have to be on your camera phone, of course. Why not take a sketchbook to commit favourite scenes to paper, or gather a collection of items along a theme? These could be patterned pebbles from a stream bed, or curious-shaped branches to create a 'stick library' at home for the dog. One of the most sublime examples of recording time well spent on a waterways wander is a collection of 60-second sound snippets from London's canals and rivers. The brainchild of the late sound recordist and archivist Ian Rawes, they included everything from rustling foliage in Barnes to buzzing insects in Hackney Marshes and were cleverly presented as a sound map of the capital's aquatic infrastructure – a sort of sonic tribute to Harry Beck's iconic Tube map.

Go with a guide

The Inland Waterways Association's Towpath Walks Society, in partnership with London Walks, has been delivering regular guided walks along London's canals since 1977. The two-hour constitutionals cover over 20 different routes, and offer something for everybody, from primary school children right up to people who have memories of the canals as working, industrial waterways. They also serve as an important fundraising stream for the charity, so you'll be giving back as well as getting clued up. Walks take place twice monthly on Sundays, starting at a Tube or DLR station, with more information at walks.com. Alternatively, the Canal & River Trust has a series of guided audio tours on its website, pointing out places of historic interest along its navigations, plus some basic mindfulness techniques to help you feel more in touch with your surroundings.

Hide and seek

Not all canal and river routes are as blindingly obvious as simply following the adjacent towpath. In London, for example, many have been hidden under centuries of development – culverted and absorbed into the city's labyrinthine sewer system – while on the canal system many became derelict and infilled following the decline of commercial carrying on them.

Tracing these old routes often requires a detective's eye for detail and can make for an incredibly satisfying stroll, but an easier option is to find someone who has done the hard graft first. Restoration societies often provide walking notes online or in pamphlets, allowing you to traipse neglected stretches as well as those that have benefited from volunteer work to bring them back into use today. Other lost watercourses, especially in London, have entire books devoted to their exploration. David Fathers' excellent guide, *London's Hidden Rivers*, is one such example, offering a choice of twelve hidden rivers to follow. He points out the traces they have left and describes some of the ways they have shaped the city. Each walk starts at the Tube or rail station nearest to the source of the river, and then follows it down to the Thames.

It would be a gross oversight to include a chapter on waterways walking without devoting a good chunk of it to the Lake District alone. The name is in fact a misnomer: only one of the 'lakes' is officially known as such in its title, Bassenthwaite Lake. The other 15 are called 'meres' or 'waters', although the distinction is often unclear (technically, a 'mere' is a lake that is really shallow in relation to its breadth, but Windermere – arguably the most famous 'mere' – is actually fairly deep).

'Tarn', however – another name for water that you'll hear bandied about in the Lakes – is something different. It indicates a small mountain lake rather than a larger valley one. Most tarns are pretty tiny, and some aren't even named.

One that is definitely worth donning walking boots for is romantic **Moss Eccles Tarn***, where the region's most famous resident, Beatrix Potter, had her rowing boat and boat house. She spent countless summer evenings either afloat or sketching along its banks, while her husband, William Heelis, was inclined to fish. Along with Esthwaite Water, it is believed to have been the inspiration for the home of her much loved character Jeremy Fisher.

Potter left Moss Eccles Tarn to the National Trust on her death, and you can find a gentle 4km (2.5-mile) walk to it described on its website (nationaltrust.org.uk/trails/beatrix-potters-moss-eccles-tarn-walk). Stick with the National Trust if you're looking for other easy waterside strolls in the area. Its Octavia Hill walk at Brandelhow Park, for example, is a nice 5.8km (3.6-mile) amble along the quiet side of **Derwent Water**, while Fell Foot's heritage and garden circular walk will take just one hour, incorporating the southern tip of **Windermere** and its historic boat houses.

If you fancy something a little quieter, consider circumnavigating **Ennerdale Water**, a glacial lake in the north-western Lake District and far from the throng of summer tourists. You'll need to allow at least four hours for this walk though, as the terrain can be challenging. Other lakes are a bit too big to tackle in their entirety in a single day. The **Ullswater Way**, for example, although easy to walk and ideal for all ages, stretches to 32km (20 miles). Perhaps concentrate on a smaller section, combined with a boat trip or bus ride, but try to incorporate the wooded section that passes below Place Fell – it is widely acknowledged to be one of the finest stretches of lakeside path in all of England.

* Adding to the bamboozling semantics of Lake District water, Alfred Wainwright argued that Moss Eccles wasn't a 'tarn' at all, but rather a reservoir, noting its absence on 19th-century maps of the area, but conceding it was 'not obtrusively artificial'. Call it what you will, I think it's a splendid spot.

Canary Wharf from the Thames Path.
(Opposite) The view from Place Fell over Ullswater.

Go the distance

Walking a river from source to sea, or a canal from end to end, can be a great challenge to set yourself. Psychologically, there's something incredibly rewarding about seeing something from start to finish, and people who have undertaken these odysseys often describe a parallel emotional journey including dealing with grief, new parenthood, unrequited love, job loss, plain boredom and countless other of life's milestones or knotty problems. By passing through so many types of settlements along the way, they're also a great way to take the pulse of a region, whether you're already familiar with it or are approaching the area as a complete stranger.

You can either do these walks all in one go, or keep returning to tackle smaller stages at a time. Some of Britain's greatest long-distance footpaths track alongside the waterways, including the Thames Path in its entirety, and Scotland's **Great Glen Way**, which stretches for 127km (79 miles) from coast to coast across the Highlands, running along the complete lengths of Loch Lochy, Loch Oich and the forests above Loch Ness, as well as along the towpath of the Caledonian Canal, the engineering marvel built by Thomas Telford that links these lochs and creates a through route from the western seaboard to the Moray Firth. The route can be walked in four to seven days and suits all levels of walker, following mainly towpaths, forest tracks and roads.

The **Thames Path**, meanwhile, follows England's undisputed queen of rivers for 296km (184 miles) from its source in the Cotswolds into the heart of London. For the sheer diversity of landscape it crawls through, the route can't be beaten. Bejewelled by historic castles and peaceful water meadows, a capital city and a string of charming towns, users are guaranteed a kaleidoscopic journey across our southern counties. Its flexibility is another factor contributing to the path's enduring appeal. Well served by public transport, pubs and places to stay, it can be enjoyed in an afternoon stroll, end-to-end trek or something in-between.

If you're a runner with long-distance ambitions, there are a number of non-stop point-to-point towpath running races. In England, the low-key '**Canalslam**' (canalrace.org.uk) comprises the Grand Union Canal Race (233km/145 miles), Kennet & Avon Canal Race (233km/145 miles) and the Leeds & Liverpool Canal Race (209km/130 miles).

ACCESS FOR ALL

The Canal & River Trust has done an excellent job of gathering information on its towpaths and their access points to make it that bit easier for everyone to discover their local waterway. An interactive map (canalrivertrust.org.uk/enjoy-the-waterways/walking/accessibility-map) lets you zoom in to find details on towpath surface, gradient and access points on to the canal. It also highlights high accessibility areas that may be suited to wheelchairs or pushchairs.

Reservoirs, meanwhile, generally have footpaths created by water companies for walkers to use, and these are often well surfaced.

In the Lake District, check out Miles without Stiles (lakedistrict.gov.uk/visiting/things-to-do/walking/mileswithoutstiles) – 50 easy-access routes suitable for those with limited mobility, wheelchairs, pushchairs or visual impairments. As the name suggests, these paths have no stiles to climb over, and are graded as suitable for some, many or all. The same website has details about accessible accommodation in the Lakes, plus residential and day activity centres.

On the Thames Path, National Trails and the Environment Agency have produced a pack of 12 walks suitable for people with reduced mobility, users of wheelchairs or mobility scooters, and people with pushchairs and young families. The walks range from near the river's source in the Cotswolds to Hampton Court on the edge of London. See visitthames.co.uk/things-to-do/walking/walks-for-all for more information.

Finally, nearly all the route of the Great Glen Way is suitable for multi-use. Many of the previous kissing gates and footbridges have been removed or replaced with more accessible alternatives.

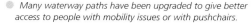

Many waterway paths have been upgraded to give better access to people with mobility issues or with pushchairs.

You don't have to like running, but at least give it a go...

It seems contrary to the spirit of this book (ways to *enjoy* the waterways, not to despise them) to admit that I hate running. Having steered clear of it for most of my life, over Christmas 2015 I found myself in a sloth of mince pies and self-loathing and, inexplicably, seized on the idea of a marathon as the answer to everything.

Along with my friend Kate, I signed up to the one in Bournemouth and, optimistically believing a seaside 42km/26-miler would be entirely flat, we concentrated most of our training efforts on similar terrain inland. At the start, this consisted mainly of short hauls along the Trent & Mersey at Fradley Junction in Staffordshire, rounded off with excellent millionaire's shortbread at the café there. Then we progressed to circumnavigating entire reservoirs. Come summer, I would spend hours at a stretch plodding alongside our narrowboat instead of in my customary position at the tiller, trying to fit in 26km (16 miles) or so before we reached our mooring for the night.

At the start, I hated it all. After a few months I only *mostly* hated it. Six years on, and still running alongside canals for no good reason, I suppose

I've learned not to mind it. Obviously, the best part is still the moment I stop, when my app serves as a metaphorical champagne pop of encouraging stats and the endorphins rinse out everything else in my head. But uniquely on a towpath, I've discovered, the interim also occasions a certain smugness thanks to the people you'll encounter along the way. On pavements, runners are a great nuisance, weaving in and out of pushchairs and commuters and wearing thin the patience of motorists at zebra crossings. On the towpath, though, runners are a source of genuine bewilderment and good-natured banter. With most other action taking place well below 4mph, you'll feel like the fastest thing on Earth overtaking that narrowboat, while the couple quaffing rosé on two fold-out chairs by the moorings will merrily tell you that Mo Farah doesn't hold a candle to you. In winter, when fewer people about necessarily means the encouraging noises are turned right down, I look to the trees to cheerlead instead. Bare but for bright balls of mistletoe in the upper branches, I easily imagine they are shaking a pom-pom of sorts, and lumber on a little happier.

A reservoir, river or lake trail lends itself well to people looking to slowly build up running fitness.

JOG YOUR MEMORY

If you need reminding why a waterways run is so good for you, the following points should spell it out:

It's great for your brain and balance

Road running lets your brain off the hook because the surface is generally smooth and straightforward. Get out on a riverbank or around a lake, however, and the uneven trail won't let you switch off in the same way. This is a more technical run, in which you'll have to pick out the best route over rocks and mud, adjusting your stride accordingly. Ground like this will also improve ankle strength, flexibility and balance. The effort of simply staying on two feet should see you welcome wonderfully strong abs…

You won't get bored

Pavements and parks can get a bit, well, same-y. Finding your nearest blue space, by contrast, offers comprehensive scene changes at least every season, plus the enduringly interesting spectacle of passing boaters and resident wildlife. Throw a bit of 'weather' into the mix and you have quite some theatre ahead. Nothing says 'good times' on a run more than getting splattered in mud, so wear it as a badge of honour.

Don't just take my word for it

Specialist mags, websites and forums are full of the wellbeing benefits of exercising outdoors and a growing number of runners have been converted to waterways routes in particular to tap into these. According to fitness app Strava, all five of the UK's most popular routes in 2020 were within striking distance of water. Two of these – along the Hertford Union and Regent's canals in London – followed waterways exclusively from start to finish.

But remember:

Watch out

Some canal bridges can be pretty low so be prepared to duck under. And keep your eyes peeled for boating/fishing paraphernalia on the towpath too – mooring pins and angling equipment are just two potential trip hazards.

Keep it leisurely

Waterside paths tend to be on the narrow side, so haring past other users is always going to feel discourteous. Maintain a steady pace and be polite about passing.

Leave your headphones at home

Although some runners prefer to be pumped up with a favourite playlist, or distracted from the pain with a podcast, unplugging every once in a while to be alone with nature and your thoughts can be a tonic. Nowhere is this more true than by water, where the clinking of windlasses and quacking of ducks offer a mellifluous soundtrack. (You'll also be able to hear other pedestrians and cyclists around you.)

Shun the traffic and embrace the space: running by water is good for mind, body and soul.

Case study

RACHEL CULLEN, MARATHON RUNNER AND AUTHOR OF *RUNNING FOR MY LIFE*

At the height of my running and racing I was more focused on the outcome than where I was choosing to run.

This changed during lockdown. I was home-schooling my then nine-year-old daughter in a small apartment. We had no outdoor space of our own so we used to head out hiking or running every weekday morning. Often this would involve water. Without consciously thinking about it our destination ended up being a reservoir, or a woodland stream, or down by the canal, and we found these places beautiful and calming.

What's happened since, and maybe because of those experiences, is that I've come to see running in a different way. I'm far more aware of the environment I'm running through, rather than simply the metadata at the end of it. It matters to me where I go.

These days I appreciate the difference between doing mile reps up and down a main road and training by water instead. Road running feels like an assault on my senses now – all the zooming traffic – whereas if I'm by water it seems to have a calming effect. Because I've had so much of the former in my running career, I appreciate these new trails so much more. I used to run listening to music on my headphones, mainly to drown out the other noise and get into my own head, but I don't do that by water. I want to be fully present in that environment, not disconnected.

I've discovered each blue space has its own vibe. The local reservoir changes depending on the weather and season. It can be quiet and soothing, while at other times the sound of the wind whipping up the water can be a really powerful thing. The canal is more consistent but there's always a bit of life buzzing around, especially when the boats are moving. I'm enjoying getting to know these places more, and making a decision before heading out on my run as to the sort of experience I crave that particular day.

'The waterways and trails around my home have saved running for me'

Basically, I feel like I'm rediscovering running in a different, and definitely a healthier, way. The waterways and trails around my home have saved running for me. After ten years of pretty hard slog and chasing PBs, I probably would have lost my love of it for good without them. Choosing where and why I'm running – and how (am I running mindfully? am I appreciating the surroundings?) – is so important and has made me enjoy my sport again. ☛ Instagram: @rachel_running_for_my_life

3 HOLIDAY AFLOAT

A stress-busting staycation at 4mph – take the helm or let someone else do the hard work

● *Canal holidays offer a chance to explore the country from a completely new perspective.*

M y first assignment on joining the editorial team of *Waterways World*, a monthly canal magazine, was to interview an elderly couple who had been hiring boats every year for half a century. At the time, having only ever endured one canal holiday as a grouchy teen with my parents, siblings, granddad, pet dog and my brother's school mate in tow, I couldn't comprehend Viv and Tony Rodgers' addiction to packed-like-sardines staycationing.

But Viv was evangelical: 'There's always something to do, a change of scenery all the time. We deliberately go at different times of year to get a different perspective. If you go to the seaside, you're stuck there. For foreign holidays, you have to get in your vehicle or get on a plane. Here, it's a great unwind from the very beginning. It's physical too, and I enjoy that. I love locking.'

Things have changed a bit since their first break back in 1965. For a start, they paid just £55. They also (and I actually wish this was still *de rigueur*) were asked to fill in a provisions list in advance of their departure, which catered for such necessities as meat paste – and boot polish. The Rodgers, I remember, requested two large tins of Ambrosia Creamed Rice as luxury extras, together with a half-bottle of Gordon's gin, their towpath tipple of choice. I thought: I like this pair. And, having hired again myself since that day, I've found I quite like boating holidays too.

The Rodgers and I aren't the only ones. Holiday hire went through the roof during the Covid pandemic as people discovered their local towpath during lockdown walks and had their curiosity whetted enough to explore them further as soon as restrictions eased. In fact, hire-boat firms began to actively market them as the perfect socially distanced break, pointing out that you're essentially in a 'bubble' the entire time.

Choosing your holiday

Narrowing down the UK's huge network of navigable inland waterways can feel overwhelming. In Scotland, there are the engineering masterpieces of the Falkirk Wheel and the Caledonian Canal to tick off; in Wales, the equally staggering Pontcysyllte Aqueduct is worth a punt. The Broads, meanwhile, is an inland sailor's paradise of lakes, rivers and idyllic market town moorings, while the main connected canal network offers another 2,000-odd miles of choice cruising.

To help you decide, consider first the disposition of your crew. If they're looking for an active holiday, heavily locked routes and/or long days at the helm will pose no problem. By contrast, if canalside beer gardens are the selling point of a boating holiday, you'll need to factor in a necessarily slower pace and routes that maximise your pub choice. Other restrictions will include the amount of time you can spare, and the type of boat you want to hire. If you desire the extra space afforded by a wide-beam canal boat, for example, your cruising will be restricted to the top and bottom of the network as it won't fit in the narrow locks elsewhere.

Once you've chosen your location, a quick internet search of hire companies along that waterway should throw up several potential operators. When making comparisons, don't just look at price. The quality of the boats is just as important, as is their size (you may not want a 21-metre/70-foot narrowboat if this is the first time you've taken the helm – but neither should you cram a family of six into something more suited to a couple). You should also check what's included in the hire price. Everything from car parking and fuel usage to bedding and the option of a 24-hour emergency call-out service could all cost extra, so do your homework well beforehand.

Finally, even though you're essentially holidaying in your backyard rather than jetting off anywhere exotic, you might still want to sort travel insurance in case of theft, injury or cancellation. The boat itself should be covered by a damage waiver in the event of any bumps or broken windows. Check the small print to make sure.

If you're physically impaired or arranging a trip for someone with a disability, take a look at some of the fantastic organisations offering breaks on specially adapted craft. CanalAbility (canalability.org.uk/), for example, has three purpose-built, fully accessible broad-beam boats letting up to 12 people explore the Rivers Stort and Lee through the Essex and Hertfordshire countryside or, on longer trips, to travel to London and take in the Grand Union Canal. Enhancements aboard include a wet room, disability toilet, ramps and lifts to enable access via wheelchair, hoist points, and fully equipped galleys to prepare your own meals.

CanalAbility offers canal boat holidays and day trips for people with disabilities.

Getting underway

Before taking the helm, make sure you're satisfied that the safety and boat briefing has been comprehensive enough to leave you feeling (semi) confident you know what you're doing. Don't be afraid to ask staff questions – no matter how stupid they sound. After all, it's best to be *au fait* with how the toilet flushes before your first bathroom emergency…

Once you're out on your own, try to remember that you're sharing the space with a host of other boaters and wildlife. When passing moored craft, slow right down to tickover – the point where the gears leave neutral and the engine has just kicked in to get you moving – or risk the ire of those aboard and a bill for their smashed crockery. Even when the coast is clear, try not to leave a wake. It can erode the banks and damage the homes of creatures living in or around the water.

But the most important piece of advice? Be prepared to rip up your itinerary. Waterways holidays aren't about racing to your next mooring or gritting your teeth at the tiller through a hailstorm. Be flexible. Rather than getting drenched, have a post-luncheon lie-down indoors, listening to the somnolent patter of rain on the steel roof. If you're stuck in a queue at the lock, catch up on some holiday reading instead of futilely counting the minutes until you might get going again. Perhaps you've fallen a little in love with the barman who served you at lunch. Go back to the same pub for dinner. And then lunch again on the way home. There's no hurry, no fixed schedule, and only good things to be gained from being open-minded about the people and places you encounter on the journey.

FAVOURITE CANAL CRUISING RINGS

Before setting off, you'll have to decide whether your cruise will follow a there-and-back route or a ring. The former has the disadvantage of going over familiar ground on the way home – which could frustrate anyone yearning for new sights, sounds and adventures. If that's the case, the following suggestions might hit the spot.

Best in show

The **Avon Ring** *(Above)* is one of the finest introductions to boating you could wish for, and you won't have to do battle with the rest of the boating world while you're there, for it's a lot quieter than other rural routes like the **Four Counties Ring**. You'll cover 174 magical kilometres (108 miles), and have the chance to cut your teeth on two river navigations as well as canals. The ring takes in some of the south-west Midlands' loveliest towns including Pershore, Worcester and Tewkesbury. But it's Stratford-upon-Avon that really steals the show. Moor

(Left) Holy Trinity Church, Stratford from the River Avon.

in the basin or on the river, take in a play, enjoy the shops, dine out – and then do it all again the next day at another theatre, different boutiques, a better brasserie...

A period piece

If history is your thing, hot-foot it around the 156km (97-mile) **Cheshire Ring**, which boasts the first canal to be built in the modern waterways era, the Bridgewater, as well as some great waterways museums in Lion Salt Works and Portland Basin Museum. If you've time to spare (two weeks is best, although it can be done in one with an experienced crew), you'll be in a better position to make the most of its varied highlights, including bustling Manchester and the dramatic heights of the Peak District. With tunnels, aqueducts and Marple Locks (said to be the most picturesque flight in the country), you'll also get your fill of diverse canal infrastructure. Take a camera for sure.

Magic from the mundane

You wouldn't judge a book by its cover, and nor should you a Midlands cruise from its unprepossessing parts (Fazeley, Atherstone, the suburbs of Coventry...). The **Warwickshire Ring** pulls plenty of rabbits out of the hat on its 167km (104-mile) course, not least the two 'canal capitals' of Braunston and Birmingham, the latter giving you a flavour of urban boating without overdoing it. The rest of the route is surprisingly rural but prepare to work hard for those views with your windlass. This is a heavily-locked route that includes the infamous 'Stairway to Heaven' – a flight of 21 at Hatton. Don't worry, there's an excellent pub there to keep your spirits up.

Up for a challenge?

The **South Pennine Ring** is also worth checking out if you've got energetic crew. While 197 locks within the space of 117km (73 miles) do not make for a relaxing holiday, and a couple of phases of the journey have to be pre-booked with the navigation authority, the pay-off is worth it. The gorgeous scenery you'll encounter is made more remarkable considering that until recently much of the route was derelict.

The restoration effort to get these waterways navigable again was tremendous, but sadly the Rochdale, Calder & Hebble, Huddersfield Narrow *(Below)* and Ashton canals remain under-boated. On the plus side, it means you're unlikely to be stuck in any queues. Nevertheless, allow three weeks to complete this ring, as you'll benefit from the occasional break from its locks.

Hard graft but stunning scenery are the hallmarks of the South Pennine Ring.

TAKE THE KIDS

You might think that adding a sulky teen or howling tot to the equation would make life in the slow lane lose some of its sedate charm. But for all the challenges and confined space, a canal boating holiday can offer a rare chance to bond with kids (and expend their energy). Plan your holiday carefully and you should find plenty to keep them occupied: from wildlife spotting to playing pirates, exploring towns and cities from new angles to learning a little history along the way. Give them the tiller and they might even teach you a thing or two…

✴ STAY SAFE All reputable hire-boat companies will ensure that children are part of the safety briefing and fit lifejackets on arrival. Parents can help by laying down a few basic ground rules (taking care when stepping on and off the boat, keeping hands and feet within the surrounds of the boat in locks and when mooring, etc). If you're planning to take babies or toddlers, think carefully about how you'll supervise them through locks when one adult is steering, the other winding paddles. This is where another pair of hands might come in handy – bring Grandma with you? In fact, one of the beauties of boating is that it can offer a great chance for extended family to get involved and share childcare duties.

⬤ (Right) *Lifejackets are strongly recommended for young children.*

(Below) *Kids can get a lot out of hire-boating breaks, especially when they're given an opportunity to crew.*

✳ CHOOSE THE ROUTE TOGETHER One way to get kids invested in the trip before you even set off is to let them help you plan the itinerary. First, decide how much physical work you want the holiday to be. Heavily locked canals are great for bigger crews and hyperactive older kids, less so for younger families. Next, think about the sort of places you want to stop off at and the activities you envisage doing en route. Towpath cycle rides are all very well if the weather's fine, but a fortnight of driving rain will keep you cooped up aboard with cabin fever unless you've got a backup plan. Combining indoor urban attractions with a backwoods adventure is often the safest solution.

✳ BE PICKY ABOUT SLEEPING ARRANGEMENTS Temporary berths created by repurposing the dining furniture are fine if you have amenable and early-rising offspring. For teenagers favouring a lie-in and personal space, having a cabin to themselves is imperative. A second bathroom isn't a bad idea either.

✳ YOU DON'T HAVE TO LEAVE THE PETS AT HOME If a fortnight away from their guinea pig is going to be a wrench, bring him along. Many hire firms will let you have pets aboard (usually dogs, of course), but it's still worth checking the literature first to confirm.

✳ DON'T LET DEVICES PROVE DIVISIVE Some parents see canal holidays as a great opportunity to tear their child away from tablets, phones and other screens. If that's the aim of the holiday, discuss leaving devices at home beforehand to avoid tantrums when afloat, or set parameters on how much online time they can have during the holiday. Hire-boat firms are increasingly geared up to cater for the digital generation with Wi-Fi systems aboard, but bear in mind that being on the move or in rural locations may never give as good or consistent reception as you're used to at home.

✳ SET SPECIFIC TASKS Give older children specific tasks to do on their holiday, such as casting off, mooring, operating locks, studying the cruising guides and, when supervised, steering. Younger kids can be charged with spotting landmarks, mileposts, bridges or wildlife.

Health benefits unpacked

Any break from the daily grind is generally going to be good for you, but there's something about a floating holiday in particular that can do wonders for mind, body and soul.

CARDIOVASCULAR FITNESS AND STRENGTH BUILDING

If you're used to an all-you-can-eat breakfast before hitting the poolside sun lounger, you're in for a shock. Waterways holidays generally aren't a sedentary option. Heaving open lock gates and tackling swing bridges will test your muscles and get your heart rate going, but the aerobic exercise should leave you feeling energised and fitter by the time you have to hand the keys back. You can help yourself further by bringing bikes along or taking evening strolls along the towpath.

STRESS RELIEF AND MOOD BOOSTING

They call inland boating 'the fastest way to slow down' – and for good reason.

With a 4mph speed limit on our canals, it's a great way to duck out of the rat race for a week or so and disconnect from the day-to-day pressures of work or home life. Focus your mind instead on the task in hand – steering an 18-metre (60-foot) boat through a genteel obstacle course of oncoming boats, humpback bridges etc. Whether you find this a mindful activity or a minefield, mastering it will leave you brimming with confidence and your brain that little bit sharper.

Greener boating

Despite lots of chatter about 'greening' our waterways, electric hire-boats are still the exception rather than the norm. On Canal & River Trust waters there's only one hire company offering electric narrowboat holidays – Castle Narrowboats (www.castlenarrowboats.co.uk) on the Mon & Brec in Wales.

Other UK operators are increasingly keen to underline the green credentials of their fleet in other ways. Anglo Welsh (www.anglowelsh.co.uk), for example, boasts eco-friendly and

cruelty-free washing-up liquids and cleaning products on board, is looking to introduce a new hybrid boat, and aims to have solar panels on all its new craft by 2030. On land, it is slowly replacing its call-out vans with electric alternatives.

Keep a cruising log

A cruising log isn't just a handy reminder of your travels, journaling can do wonders for your health too – providing a release from the stresses of everyday life, or just a safe way to vent frustration at inept crew members. At the very least, it can make entertaining reading for the rest of the family. Textile legend William Morris discovered just that when, in 1880, he recorded a week-long boat trip ferrying his family, a housemaid, and four friends from his London home in Hammersmith to Kelmscott Manor near Lechlade. The 12-page log, now kept in the British Library, was circulated among his passengers, with pencil marks on the backs of pages made in various hands. One addendum, by Morris's daughter Jenny, claims the single 'noteworthy feature of this journey was, that everybody perpetually gave orders in a very loud voice, and that nobody ever paid the slightest attention to them'. Family holidays, it seems, have changed little over the course of a century.

Thanks to social media and better word-processing software, diarising your movements doesn't have to be a sterile list of miles covered and locks encountered. TikTok videos of your other half tackling a swing bridge and hashtag-no-filter Insta posts of dreamy sunsets over the Broads have added personality – and reach – to log entries in recent years. Others still prefer good old-fashioned pen and paper, but keep things colourful with Polaroids or sketches of scenes they don't want to forget.

Whatever your medium, a quick word on content. Obviously cruising stats still have a place, but daily comments could also include wildlife sightings, pub reviews and funny things that have happened en route. Bear in mind, however, that recording the 'comedy' of it all will require a little more effort than simply renaming your crew 'The Captain' et al, or dousing your paragraphs with exclamation marks and LOLs, so get creative.

A self-drive hire-boat over the Pontcysyllte Aqueduct on the Llangollen Canal.

ALTERNATIVE WATERWAYS BREAKS

Self-drive boating breaks aren't for everyone, but before ruling out a waterways vacation wholesale, take a look through the following ideas for something more suited to your palate and/or price range.

Put up your feet on a hotel-boat

If you're not keen on cooking and steering yourself, hotel-boating *(Right)* offers a more pampered introduction to floating holidays. You'll necessarily pay more for the experience (around £1,000 per person for a six-night break on northern waterways; more than triple that for a suite on the Thames) but expect five-star service from most operators. The craft themselves are also a cut above – you won't have to leave your hair straighteners at home, for instance, lest the power draw drains the batteries. Here you can plug in the iPad, pop on the kettle and put in a couple of rounds of toast simultaneously. It's the boating dream.

Volunteer for a coal run

If hiring a boat is going to blow your budget, there are other, cheaper ways to get afloat. The Narrow Boat Trust (narrowboattrust.org.uk) actively seeks volunteer 'crew' to sustain its canal-carrying operations *(Below)*. It runs the working pair Nuneaton (a motor) and Brighton (a butty) in an effort to recapture a time when our canals were a heavy haulage route rather than a holiday playground. The boats cruise south twice a year laden with up to 40 tons of coal, delivering to various locations on the Grand Union, the Oxford, the River Wey, the Kennet & Avon and

(Left) *Lengthman's Cottage on the Stratford Canal.*

(Far left) *Staff serve morning tea to hotel-boat guests on the Bridgewater Canal.*

(Bottom left) *Combine a holiday afloat with helping out on a Narrow Boat Trust coal run.*

the Thames. Conditions aboard can be spartan and crew are expected to work the boats, navigate the locks and load/ unload the coal by hand, living in each other's pockets all the while. But there aren't many opportunities to spend time away from the modern world, living as you would have done a century ago, and getting involved won't cost you anything save for the price of membership to the Narrow Boat Trust.

Unwind in a waterside holiday let

The internet is saturated with ads for waterside properties, including the Landmark Trust's Lengthsman's Cottage at Lowsonford on the Stratford Canal. This charming barrel-roofed property dates from 1812, sleeps four, and is just a stone's throw from all the boating action at Lock 31.If you'd rather be *lough*side, head to County Fermanagh and an unbeatably romantic thatched-cottage-and-gypsy-caravan set-up beside Lough Erne. With a 1950s-style interior, Geaglum Cottage is billed as one of the best preserved in Northern Ireland. Even better, it's located less than half a mile from a little-used shingle beach and the maze of waterways and islets beyond, ticking all the boxes for watersports fans.

Come home qualified

Bear Boating (bearboating.co.uk) on the Leeds & Liverpool Canal offers a novel chance to holiday afloat while receiving instruction towards an RYA Inland Waterways Helmsman qualification, making it a great option for novice – or nervous – boaters. An instructor will join you during the first day's cruise along your chosen route, slowly building up your knowledge and skills. Come 5pm they'll leave you safely moored up and free to enjoy your sundowner – or swot up on the next day's syllabus. On day two, as soon as you've satisfied the required competencies you'll be left to enjoy the rest of your holiday in peace.

Get adventurous

For the antithesis of a staid canal boat sojourn, head to North Wales and a company called Adventure Tours UK (adventuretoursuk.com). It offers an eight-day, adrenaline-pumped taster of the region's best outdoor experiences, from mountain hiking and coasteering to, more pertinently, white-water rafting on the River Dee and kayaking on Snowdonia's Llyn Padarn. You'll need to be fit, active, 18 or over and probably deranged. But good luck to you. For those of a calmer bent there's also a 'Wild Wellness Retreat', which incorporates paddleboarding and collecting eggs from the site's resident hens.

Case study

SIR DAVID SUCHET, ACTOR AND CANAL CAMPAIGNER

A few years ago my wife and I decided, in the middle of a very hectic schedule, to take three weeks out. I managed to find a hire-boat company in the north of England to rent me a boat for that period, on the Leeds & Liverpool Canal. We started near Barnoldswick and headed towards Leeds, across the Pennines. It provided some of the most beautiful scenery I've ever experienced in my life. It was so stunning that we decided to go slow – slow even by narrowboating standards – and really drink it up. I was photographing it while Sheila got out her watercolours, and we did some walking. And the time, three weeks, flew by, and we never made it back to Liverpool.

I have two things on my bucket list, as far as future canal holidays are concerned. The first is to go from Barnoldswick to Liverpool, because I want to do the rest of that waterway. It may not be as pretty, but it's still part of our incredible waterways network and I love the industrial cities, and seeing all that heritage from the water. The canal network is the only facility we have that was once so entirely focused on transport and communications and moving goods around, and is now essentially a playground. After that, I'd love to hire in Scotland and see the Falkirk Wheel.

Until recently I was lucky enough to live overlooking the water. Returning home from the West End after a heavy show, I'd always take a few minutes to drink in the view, whatever the weather. If it was cold I'd put on a coat and lean over the balcony with a cup of tea and just look at the water. There's something wonderful about that. You can calm down and let go. Water does that to me. It just takes away all the stress and tension.

Expanded from an interview in *Waterways World*, June 2020, with that magazine's kind permission.

'It just takes away all the stress and tension'

4 GO FISHING

Reel one in, catch your thoughts, or lark about on the foreshore looking for buried treasure

G rowing up, I used to think the phrase 'with bated breath' must have its etymology in fishing. In my head it was always '*baited* breath' and the entire sport of angling has consequently been coloured, for me, by the mental image of a mouthful of maggots and huge excitement.

Of course, I now know that bated breath has more to do with abated breathing than champing grubs. But fishing's association with nervous energy hasn't gone away. If anything, trying out the sport as an adult only confirmed the childish notion. Turning up at one of the Angling Trust's brilliant free Get Fishing taster sessions on the bank of the Trent & Mersey Canal one gloomy Sunday morning was a genuine thrill. Three roach, two perch and a bucketful of psychedelic pink larvae later, I was still pumped.

Which is an odd reaction, you might think, for a pastime that's 95 per cent sitting on your bum in an anorak for hours at a time – in rainy old Blighty, at least. But the thing about fishing – and this is what makes it so pertinent to waterways-induced wellbeing – is that the lack of what sticklers might call 'action' is more than made up for by the quality time spent lounging about in your mind and in nature, or in idle chat with a friend who's come along with you.

As a child, 'going fishing' legitimises adventure. It's something you tell your mum as you walk out of the door with a mate to fetch your bikes and hare off down to the river for a day of happy serendipity, loosely hung around fiddling with tackle but often also incorporating minor trespass, getting your sandwiches nicked and other coming-of-age staples.

As an adult, 'going fishing' offers a similar opportunity to loosen up. Chris Yates, the angling writer and presenter par excellence, once wrote that the kind of fishing he does is really 'just like dreaming', and he's spot on. It's licence to let your mind wander and cook up all sorts of fantasies about the size of your next catch or if the weather will hold for a swift half in the beer garden on the way home.

This dreaming can be a solitary thing, but many anglers prefer to 'burble' (Yates's perfect verb) about fish and all sorts of other topics with a pal instead. Indeed, fishing with another person is a good way to make, rekindle or repair relationships over a shared passion. Many anglers recount stories of childhoods with otherwise distant dads, where fishing offered rare closeness without the awkwardness of conversation. This bumping along shoulder to shoulder (rather than a face-to-face interrogation) is also why so many people find it easier to talk about difficult subjects on a riverbank rather than in traditional therapy, and why social prescribing of the sport has soared.

Back to Chris Yates for a second – please do read a couple of his angling books if you have any lingering doubts about the lure of fishing. His sentences, more than any others, explain the magic of it all, from the 'sweet greenhouse air' that hangs over still water on a summer night to the copious tea-drinking and #picnicgoals of fruit loaf and bramble jelly.

Alternatively, watch a few episodes of the effortlessly charming *Mortimer & Whitehouse: Gone Fishing*. Bob Mortimer will swear blind that he's not an angler in terms of technique, using all the gear, or catching the most fish. But he is, he says, a GREAT fisherman when it comes to the enjoyment he gleans from it. In a book that accompanies the series, he suggests all anglers should be put on some sort of machine afterwards that can quantify how good a time they've had. Whoever scores top for having had the loveliest day, 'that's the best fisherman', he says. I think about that when I'm sitting with my four-year-old beside our local waterway with little more than a growing pile of Interesting Wet Leaves to show for our efforts. I doubt a brown trout will ever swim into the purse of our net, its belly burning gold in the sun. But we're still the best on the river – and you can be too.

Getting started

First, you'll need to get your head around the basic types of fishing. Coarse fishing is the most common form of freshwater angling in Britain's rivers, lakes and canals. Anything caught is safely returned to the water – traditionally because the fish being hunted were deemed unfit to eat. Coarse fish generally have larger scales and tend to be found in warmer, stiller waters.

If you're after more palatable salmon or trout, that's game fishing and the technique you'd usually use is called fly fishing.

Let's stick with coarse fishing here, for simplicity's sake. You'll hear lots of different techniques described online and by other anglers, but the main ones are pole and whip fishing, lure fishing, float fishing, and ledgering. Each requires different rods, reels and tackle, so your best bet is to join one of the Angling Trust's Get Fishing taster sessions or, in conjunction with the Canal & River Trust, Let's Fish events. They take place throughout the country, with further details online: anglingtrust. net/getfishing/ and canalrivertrust.org. uk/enjoy-the-waterways/fishing/lets-fish. You can borrow tackle and bait and get to pick the brains of more experienced anglers. Other options include signing up for beginner sessions at your local angling club, or just tagging along with someone who knows what they're doing. Online tutorials, of which there are masses, can also help.

If you like it, you'll want to invest in your own tackle. You can buy a basic fishing set-up for about £25, and the key really is to keep things simple at the beginning. Specialist retailers will be able to offer advice on what you do and don't need. Waterproofs should also be on your kit list.

Once you've been shown the technique and got the gear, it's really a waiting game. This time can be a wonderful antidote to the short attention span we're unconsciously cultivating in other areas of 21st-century life, where apps and social media feeds relentlessly fight for our focus. Just sit back, have a cuppa, and watch your line carefully. You'll feel it jerk forward when something bites. Wait to let any slack out before reeling in the fish.

Once your catch is in hand, there's just one more dark art of angling to learn: how to make the fish look bigger for the photo. Top tip: hold it horizontal, with your arms stretched out in front of you and hidden behind the fish if possible. Try to shoot slightly up at the fish. And smile, by all means, but make it a *strained* smile. This monster is *heavy*.

Where to do it

Commercial lakes and the manicured banks of chalk streams are all very well, but there's nothing wrong with getting started on your local canal.

Look for spots with reeds, logs and rocks, which provide food and plenty of cover when fish feel threatened. If there are currents, look for spots in the water where the faster- and slower-moving ones meet. Many fish will lurk here to catch food drifting past. If you end up in a spot where the fish aren't biting, give it 15 minutes before trying somewhere else.

Most importantly, however, choose a place that you won't mind staying at for several hours. Make sure you're not crossing private property, however, or fishing on a site that doesn't allow it. And take care not to cause too much disturbance to the local flora and fauna on the bank.

You won't need too many complicated bits of tackle or baits to fish on canals. One angler I spoke to recalled making do with a slice of bread and spoonful of sugar as a youngster, which he called 'bread paste'.

Canals contain the whole size range of fish, and with no particular expertise you will probably get bites all day from ones ranging from 7.5cm (3in) long to 15–20cm (6–8in) long. Look for roach, perch, chub, pike and carp in particular, and there is even a flowing stretch of the Kennet & Avon Canal where grayling are sometimes caught.

Bear in mind that the best fishing is either early or late in the day when there is less bankside disturbance, the boats have stopped and the locks are not operating and therefore creating moving water. Salmon fishers tend to gravitate to Scotland, where the Tay, Tweed, Spey and lesser known, less accessible River Carron in the Highlands hold court. However, don't overlook other locations in the UK – Dartmoor, the Wye and the Tyne all have wild landscapes and hungry fish, as well as fishing prices that won't break the bank.

Licences and permits

Before you start fishing in England or Wales, you'll need to buy a rod licence. Don't let this put you off – you can do it easily enough online (gov.uk/fishing-licences/buy-a-fishing-licence) or at the post office. They start from £30 a year (you can also buy one-day and eight-day licences for £6 and £12 respectively). Under-13s don't need a licence, and 13- to 16-year-olds can register online for free. If you're fishing on private land, you'll also need the landowner's permission.

Fishing rights to most of the inland waterways network belong to local fisheries or angling clubs. Sometimes you'll be able to buy a one-day licence from a bailiff, but others demand you join as a member and pay an annual subscription. Check the Angling Trust website (anglingtrust.net) for further details.

On the canal network, stretches that haven't been rented to local angling clubs can be fished with a Waterway Wanderers permit from the Canal & River Trust (canalrivertrust.org.uk). Expect to pay from £23 a year as an adult, or £5 if you're aged 16 or under.

You do not need a licence to fish with rod and line anywhere in Scotland apart from in the Border Esk region – only permission from the landowner or an angling club. You'll need a rod licence in Northern Ireland, however. Depending on where you want to fish, contact DAERA (daera-ni.gov.uk) or the Loughs Agency (loughs-agency.org). You must also have a permit from the fishery owner.

With so many types of freshwater fish in the UK, getting started in angling can often feel overwhelming. Better to choose one or two to focus on. Research their preferred habitats and how best to catch them, including suitable bait to lure them in. The five species below are commonly coarse fished and should help you begin:

PERCH

CARP

PIKE

BARBEL

ROACH

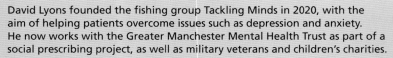

David Lyons founded the fishing group Tackling Minds in 2020, with the aim of helping patients overcome issues such as depression and anxiety. He now works with the Greater Manchester Mental Health Trust as part of a social prescribing project, as well as military veterans and children's charities.

How did you first get into fishing?
I took it up as a child, aged four or five. I used to go with my older brother and cousin. We fished in the summer mainly, and this carried on until my late teens. Then life got in the way, and for one reason or another I only returned to it relatively recently, aged 37. But it was always there. I never lost that love for the sport.

What prompted you to take it up again?
I was struggling with my mental health, which had unfortunately led to alcohol addiction. In the five years before returning to fishing I was in and out of detoxes – four to date. I never had anything to look forward to, never felt mentally ready to jump back into work. I had no motivation or direction. I lost that buzz for life, I suppose. Something just wasn't right.

Then I moved into a new place, which overlooked a lake, and it was exactly the kick I needed to get back into fishing. Just getting outside again and engaging with other people was better than any medication or therapy I'd tried. I figured, if fishing works for me, why not other people as well? And that's how Tackling Minds came about – initially just by telling other people my story on Facebook. Before I knew it, thousands of people were following and sharing their experiences too.

What sort of people come along to the sessions?
We get everybody. We work with army veterans, a lot of whom have PTSD, and a lot of people are referred to us from different departments within the NHS, as well as children's charities like Barnardo's. Anyone can come. Some have already fished, and it's always great when it brings back memories. But 70 per cent of the people who come angling with us have never tried it before. Some insist they don't want to try, and would rather stand on the bank watching, but before you know it they're fishing and they're usually the last ones to leave!

What is it about fishing that makes it easier for people to open up about their struggles?
You're in an environment where you're not necessarily having to make eye contact, so it feels less threatening I suppose. You're sitting down, relaxed, with something else to fall back on – the fishing – if there are awkward silences or the conversation stumbles.

Do you still find time to fish recreationally, rather than through Tackling Minds?
Yes, usually on a local river or canal, and I always go with friends. We go out even in winter, mainly pike fishing. This weekend we're meeting on the canal in Manchester. We'll have a bit of a natter, get our gear together and spend most of the day there. Pike fishing is quite an active form of angling. You're often seeking out the fish in different spots in the water, so you're not just sitting down all day. It's a great form of mild exercise, especially if you're coming back from an injury or are an elderly angler.

Your tagline for Tackling Minds is: 'Fishing is not a sport, it's a way of life'. How much of that is true in your own life?
Tackling Minds has really taken over my life, so fishing is essentially my job now. It spills into my social life too, as I still enjoy it as a hobby. Fishing can consume a lot of your time. You have to prepare for the type of fish you're going after, get your bait and tackle ready, and my WhatsApp groups are full of talk about upcoming outings. Ask my girlfriend and she'd probably say fishing takes up too much of my life, but I think I've got a good balance!

☛ tacklingminds.org

Case study

LEONIE PATERSON, RECREATIONAL ANGLER

Although I'd dabbled in sea fishing during childhood holidays, it wasn't until I met my husband that I tried freshwater fishing. Our first trip was to the Lake District to fish for anything that we could catch – which turned out to be nothing. But I quickly realised that wasn't the point. Being at one with nature, focusing on not a lot, quiet comfortable company, mastering the casting – and waiting in anticipation that things could change at any minute. This is the stuff that counts. For me, fishing is the definition of hope.

We started fly fishing in our 50s as our children grew independent and we had more time to contemplate our navels. We have visited the most stunning scenery with time to stand and really look, while being immersed in the techniques of chucking small bits of fluff on the end of a long fishing line. Alongside this we have continued to pike fish, canal fish, any fish really, which has fostered endless patience and relaxed enjoyment in all water environments.

I enjoy watching cricket: the next ball may be spectacular, or the next, or the hundredth after that. Fishing is the same. Just one fish and I'll be happy. Then that magical tug, a frisson of excitement as you hook something, the care and skill to land a fish safely. How beautiful they are, especially the brown trout. And then seeing them return to the wild with all the grace and power they possess. Afterwards, I always think I'd just like one more fish... It's *all* about the hope!

'Fishing is the definition of hope'

Fishing for treasure

If you don't have the patience, tackle or technique for traditional fishing, there are other ways to trawl our waterways. Mudlarking may well conjure images of Victorian urchins 'grimed with the foul soil of the river', as the social reformer Henry Mayhew so desperately put it, but these days riverside scavenging has been massively gentrified by a new tribe of hip, Instagramming history nuts, whose finds have spawned grid envy and bestselling books by the bucketload.

Leading the charge to the Thames foreshore are the likes of Lara Maiklem (@london.mudlark) and Ted Sandling (@tedsandling). Lara says it was a search for peace and quiet amid the chaos of the city that initially led her down to the river, but the discovery of a section of clay pipe piqued her curiosity and kept her coming back. It is, she says in her TEDx Talk on the subject (www.ted.com/talks/lara_maiklem_trash_or_historical_artifact), 'a place where history becomes real'. Ted agrees. When I interviewed him for the River Thames Society in 2016, he conceded that you can see most of the objects he's found on the foreshore in museums, usually in a better state. But there is a big difference, he pointed out, between viewing them 'stifled' behind glass and holding something in your hand, having just plucked it out of the mud.

Wannabe Thames mudlarks will need to apply for a permit from the Port of London Authority (pla.co.uk/Environment/Thames-foreshore-permits) before treasure hunting, which costs £96 and lasts three years. Before shelling out, it might be useful to join a guided foreshore walk to see if you like it. Wear wellies and bring antibacterial handwash, a couple of plastic bags and a trowel (permits allow you to dig up to 7.5cm). You should be aware of the tides too, and know how to get off the river

quickly when the water starts to rise.

Magnet fishing is no less popular a pastime, even counting England rugby ace James Haskell among its fans. Like mudlarking, participants have hauled out their fair share of historic relics, although modern-day gadgets and mangled bicycles are more likely.

You can pick up a decent magnet with an eyebolt (for the rope) from about £30, and a complete starter kit (including rope, magnet case, gloves and carabiner) from £100. Then it's simply a case of throwing the magnet into the water, letting it sink, and seeing what you can slowly pull out.

Although magnet fishers point out that they're effectively cleaning up our waterways, many navigation authorities forbid it on their networks, including the Canal & River Trust. They argue the hobby is inherently dangerous, because 'items dragged out by magnets could be sharp or heavy and cause you to be dragged into the water'. Periodic reports of people fishing out old war bombs and dumped weapons don't help matters.

To magnet fish on Scotland's canal network, you must have Scheduled Monument Consent from Historic Environment Scotland and permission from the landowners, Scottish Canals. You can get around this by joining Official Magnet Fishing Scotland (facebook.com/groups/officialmagnetfishingscotland/), which has all the paperwork already in place to magnet fish between Leamington Lift Bridge and Hermiston Aqueduct on the Union Canal in Edinburgh. The group are also in the process of applying for further consents in both Glasgow and Inverness.

Items pulled from the water should be disposed of properly and not thrown back in. Hand weapons to the police and, where something obviously belongs to someone and is clearly marked, 'fishermen' are obliged to try and contact the legal owner. A useful tip is to wear gloves, to avoid injury not just from rusty, sharp metal, but from waterborne diseases and rope burn too.

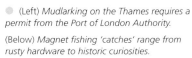

(Left) *Mudlarking on the Thames requires a permit from the Port of London Authority.*

(Below) *Magnet fishing 'catches' range from rusty hardware to historic curiosities.*

5 PACK A PICNIC

Recreate Ratty's feast on the riverbank, take your food afloat, or dine for free on foraged fare

Our picnic hamper doubles as my son's dressing-up basket, and there's something rather apt about it being appropriated like this when it comes to waterside feasts. Getting the food ready in itself can often feel like a performance, but the real theatre, the kick-back-and-soak-it-all-up stuff, comes once you've laid out the blanket, unpacked the victuals and poured the first drink. On our canals, there's a word for this activity – to leisurely watch the parade of boats and wildfowl while ensconced on the nearest bank or in a beer garden – 'gongoozling'. And I've always thought it makes whatever you're scoffing or quaffing at the time taste better.

There could be a scientific reason for this as, evolutionarily, we're programmed to relax in nature. In a food context, feeling calmer gives us the mental space to pay proper attention to what we're eating, so we savour it that bit more. In addition, given that most people only picnic very occasionally, we feel liberated from the constraints of a dining table and tend to enter into the novelty of al fresco meals with a bit more gusto.

For many, picnics also tap into childhood nostalgia. Food writer Di Murrell, author of *A Foodie Afloat*, a cookbook cum memoir inspired by an inland waterways voyage through France, says our rose-tinted memories of sunny summer feasts rarely reflect the reality of 'soggy tomatoes sandwiched between slices of Mother's Pride and a sausage roll one had inadvertently sat on on the coach', yet we still recall picnics with affection. They feel playful, less formal, exciting – even if our palates have necessarily developed as adults. 'Wiser with age,' Di continues, 'one enters a more sophisticated phase – where picnics start with oysters and river-cooled Chablis. There follow feasts of cold cuts, salads, pastries and rosé wine, raspberries, cream and a burnt orange trifle to finish.'

I can't say my picnic provender has ever reached such dizzy culinary heights, but it doesn't spoil the fun. The wonderful thing about eating in the great outdoors is that aiming for perfection is pretty futile anyway – it's more about going with the flow. If your lakeside

sandwiches are a little gritty from the sand, or the napkins keep running away on the breeze off the water, so be it. There's something about these minor frustrations that serves as a useful reminder that nature is beyond our control. And maybe it's because of these trials, or maybe just too much ginger ale in the sun, that after a good waterways picnic the rest of the day feels somehow quite easy.

Corkscrews
and venues

Menu choices can be fluid, but spare a thought for basic picnicking hardware to pack alongside the foodstuffs. An early edition of *Mrs Beeton's Book of Household Management* advocates three corkscrews, although admittedly her spread is for 40 people and includes such abundant booze as six bottles of sherry, six bottles of claret, champagne 'at discretion' and two bottles of brandy.

In terms of venue, your local waterway should have plenty of beauty spots that recommend themselves, but you might want to filter out any that are too far from public WCs or a car park (if you're carrying heavy hampers). Waterways Ireland lists some great spots for waterside picnics on its website (waterwaysireland.org/10-great-picnic-areas), including at **Toome Linear Park** on the shores of the Lower Bann where it runs into Lough Neagh. There are lovely walks along this river to work up an appetite first, and plenty of benches if you haven't brought a rug to loll on. In England and Wales, check out the Canal & River Trust's suggestions (canalrivertrust.org.uk/news-and-views/features/perfect-places-for-picnics) or pick out some waterside recommendations on *Countryfile*'s list of Britain's best picnic spots (countryfile.com/go-outdoors/days-out/britains-best-picnic-spots), like **Lydford Gorge** in Devon or **Bowlees Picnic Area**, Durham.

Finally, do remember to check the weather forecast in advance and always take home any litter with you afterwards.

Waterside snacks and a sundowner on the Thames.

Floating feasts

Not all picnics have to be confined to bankside buffets – there are plenty of boat-hire firms offering a chance to eat afloat. **GoBoat** (goboat.co.uk) (*Right*), for example, offers eco-friendly electric self-drive craft seating up to eight people around a sociable table. Locations include Paddington, Canary Wharf and Kingston-upon-Thames, and boats are available for up to three hours.

On the Norfolk Broads you can book afternoon tea aboard one of **Herbert Woods**' picnic boats (herbertwoods. co.uk) at Potter Heigham. These craft seat nine and include a gas hob for making tea and coffee, plus a small fridge. The cream tea hamper, which comes with a £25 surcharge, consists of a Victoria sponge cake, home-made sausage rolls, fruit scones with clotted cream, butter and jam, home-made cheese scones with Cheddar cheese and onion chutney, and fresh fruit.

Alternatively, opt for a skippered cruise, such as on the River Dee in Chester. **ChesterBoat** (chesterboat. co.uk) charges £150 for up to five passengers for a 90-minute cruise (the perfect length, it says, to see the highlights of the Dee). You'll need to pack your own food but you can pre-book drinks to have them chilled and waiting.

If you want something a little more substantial than finger food, the waterways network has plenty of floating restaurants. In London you'll be especially spoilt for choice with the **Cheese Barge** (www.thecheesebar.com/paddington/), **London Shell Company** (londonshellco.com), **Caravel @ Studio Kitchen** (thestudiokitchen.co.uk/the-boat/), **Barge East** (www.bargeeast. com), **Feng Shang Princess** (www. fengshang.co.uk) and **Daisy Green** (www.daisygreenfood.com/locations), which offer the full range of dining

● (Above) *Picnic afloat on one of GoBoat's electric hire-craft.*

(Below) *Bristol's Grain Barge offers locally-sourced dishes and a range of craft beers, ciders, wines and coffees.*

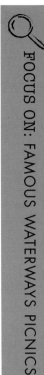

Visions of Ratty's capacious hamper in *The Wind in the Willows* have stayed with most of us since childhood and it's hard to find more mouth-watering contents than those he rattles off without pausing for breath – or punctuation:

'What's inside it?' asked the Mole, wriggling with curiosity.
'There's cold chicken inside it,' replied the Rat briefly:
'coldtonguecoldhamcoldbeefpickledgherkinssaladfrenchrollscresss andwichespottedmeatgingerbeerlemonadesodawater–'
'Oh stop, stop!' cried the Mole in ecstasies. *'This is too much!'*
'Do you really think so?' enquired the Rat seriously. *'It's only what I always take on these little excursions; and the other animals are always telling me that I'm a mean beast and cut it very fine.'*

By contrast, Jerome K Jerome's waterway classic *Three Men in a Boat* provides an epic picnic *fail* in the form of a tin of pineapple – and the cruel absence of any tool to open it. After trying all sorts of increasingly desperate (but progressively funnier) hacks, the saga ends with it being flung into the middle of the river. 'As it sank we hurled our curses at it, and we got into the boat and rowed away from the spot, and never paused till we reached Maidenhead.'

For the dreamiest riverside lunch in all of literature, however, we have to consult a fairly obscure canoeing travelogue called *The Heart of England by Waterway* (1933) by William Bliss. His solitary meal on the banks of the Oxford Canal is a triumph of simplicity and freak weather. Not only is his menu necessarily pared back by the lack of space in his boat, but he's also paddling out of season – March or early April, with a north-west wind 'and even a few flakes of snow' when he set off that morning. What follows is nothing short of an Easter miracle then:

As I let my canoe come to rest against the sheltering bank a heavenly scent of Spring came to me on the sun-warmed wind, and I looked up at the bank to see, just above my right shoulder, a colony of white violets. I had found Spring and would celebrate the discovery. I had provided for lunch, I remember, a fillet steak, cooked over-night and cold, with bread and salt and a bottle of Burgundy. I do not remember ever to have enjoyed a better meal. Sun and water and a Cotswold wind and beef and Burgundy and white violets and the young Cherwell running happily down there three fields away between pollard willows and osiers flushed red with Spring, and over on the other side of the valley, where the hills rose again, the square tower of a church and village roofs among trees – elms purplish with flower. That was good enough, I thought, even if it snowed again before I got to Banbury.

experiences to suit every palate and budget. Elsewhere, Bristol's **Grain Barge** (grainbarge.com) (*Left*), which started life carrying barley and wheat across the Severn Estuary, serves a veg-focused and seafood menu and is worth checking out. Meanwhile, Edinburgh has **Fingal** (fingal.co.uk) – a stylish hotel and restaurant aboard a former Northern Lighthouse Board ship. The art deco dining room features leather seats, wood panelling and floor-to-ceiling windows, which look out on to the Firth of Forth.

WATERSIDE EATERIES TO WHET YOUR APPETITE

Leave the blanket and hamper at home, if you like. In the UK we're spoilt for choice when it comes to waterside dining options, with a glut of cafés, pubs and even Michelin-starred restaurants flanking our rivers, lakes and canals.

Towpath (towpathlondon.com) on the Regent's Canal in Hackney, London is one of my favourites. Operating from four unprepossessing kiosks directly on to the towpath, chef Laura and front of house Lori have created a veritable canal institution built on unfussy seasonal menus, prettily dressed al fresco tables and a warm welcome. You can try recreating something of their success in your own home with a copy of their excellent cookbook, simply called *Towpath*. Recipes are arranged according to the café's 'year' (it's only open from March to November).

Heading north, **Chesters by the River** (chestersbytheriver.co.uk) at Skelwith Bridge near Ambleside, Cumbria also claims to be a café, but offers a cut above the normal fare. Take a walk to Skelwith Force first, one of the smaller Lake District waterfalls, before indulging in a lazy lunch on the riverside terrace. You can

also take away or pick up stuff from the shop, but it's best to hang around and enjoy the buzzy vibe, predominantly vegan menu and fantastic views with a proper sit-down meal.

Finally, to Loch Fyne on Scotland's west coast, where **Inver** (Below) (inverrestaurant.co.uk) offers seafood and native meat and game in season, with delicious views of the bobbing boats and distant mountains from large picture windows. The restaurant is a regular on best-in-Britain lists and even offers accommodation in luxury, en-suite bothies to sleep off any overindulgence.

Smoked Trout, Watercress & Horseradish Sandwich

Cress sandwiches have been a staple of waterside picnics for aeons. The aquatic herb was first commercially cultivated in 1808 along the River Ebbsfleet in Kent. These days the unquestionable capital of cress activity is the town of Alresford near Winchester, on the River Alre. Not only does it hold an annual Watercress Festival, it also boasts a preserved steam railway line named after the local crop.

The following recipe for six sandwiches comes courtesy of hotel-boat chef Gael Robertson:

- 125g cream cheese
- 1tbsp creamed horseradish
- 12 slices of wholemeal or rye bread
- 175g sliced smoked trout
- 75g watercress

Mix the cream cheese with the horseradish and spread liberally on each slice of bread. Place the smoked trout and watercress on half of the bread, and top with the remaining slices.

Inver restaurant on the shores of atmospheric Loch Fyne.

71

Waterways foraging

Some of the best waterside picnics are impromptu snacks on stuff you've picked straight from nature. Almost as much as I like doing this myself, I like reading poems about other people's experiences. There is a whole canon of poetry about foraging – from Seamus Heaney and Sylvia Plath's blackberrying, to Mimi Khalvati's 'Picking Raspberries with Mowgli' and Genevieve Taggard's 'Millions of Strawberries'. What they have in common is a sense of the strange mania that comes with foraging – a 'lust' as Taggard put it, and Heaney uses the same yearn-y, sensuous word.

Lots of articles online and in books will tell you that foraging reconnects us with nature, and it does, wonderfully. We discover how food grows and how to use it efficiently, and the process of feeding ourselves from the plants we find on or near our doorstep can enhance our sense of place.

But foraging, I think, also reconnects us with *our* nature. Not just our hunter gatherer ancestry but, if we are to believe the poets, something almost carnal. How it feels on our fingers, and can ink our skin and lips, and the soft swell of it in our basket is plain sexy in verse. In real life, if not always quite so aphrodisiacal, it still taps into something wild in all of us. I don't know if foraging next to water makes this any more intense, but it's certainly preferable to roadside picking where passing cars will only herd us back to unwelcome sobriety.

Foraging can also feel like a small, satisfying act of empowerment, a reclaiming of the environment from the industrial food systems that pillage and profit from it. And as the cost of living continues to soar, you won't need reminding that this food is completely free.

WHAT TO LOOK FOR

Our inland waterways provide plenty of foraging opportunities if you know what to look for and when. But pick with discretion – it's polite to leave some for others, including the local wildlife.

WILD GARLIC (also known as ransoms) makes an excellent introduction to waterways foraging. It is easy to find in shady, damp sites, and quickly identifiable by its strong scent, green pointed leaves and white flowers. Start looking for it in late winter until the end of spring. It's the leaves you're after (don't uproot the bulbs) – these can be chopped and used like garlic for flavouring, or blended with walnuts, olive oil and Parmesan to make a pesto. The flowers, meanwhile, make a good-looking edible decoration on savoury dishes.

ELDERFLOWER
Late May to June is the best time to collect creamy white ELDERFLOWERS in towpath hedgerows. Cut the flower heads just below where the small stems meet the main stem, and take care to only gather a few from each tree: the berries that form later are an important food source for birds, mammals and insects. The flowers can be added to cakes or biscuits, or used to make elderflower cordial, fritters or even sorbet.

BLACKBERRIES

Few fruits are more synonymous with British summer than BLACKBERRIES in August, September and even into October. Rifling through the brambles beside our rivers, lakes and canals usually offers easy pickings as they love having their feet in the water and heads in the sun. Back at home, wash the berries well in cold water and eat them quickly – they lose flavour and condition fast. If you've too many, freeze the surplus for crumbles and pies over winter.

WILD APPLES

WILD APPLES are also plentiful along British canals, but often get overlooked. Just remember to cut them up to check for grubs before eating. The sweeter ones are perfect for your fruit bowl, while more sour-tasting specimens should be set aside for cakes and puddings.

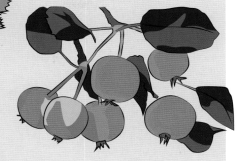

PLUMS AND DAMSONS

Finally, September and October usually bring a glut of PLUMS and DAMSONS along our inland waterways. Extremely versatile, you can eat them as they are, or pop them in wines, jams and crumbles.

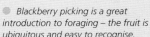

● Blackberry picking is a great introduction to foraging – the fruit is ubiquitous and easy to recognise.

Case study

My dream was always academia more than cooking, and I was well on my way to completing a Masters in Shakespearean Literature when a head injury put a spanner in the works. Impaired vision and chronic neuralgia made reading near impossible, and it was our narrowboat which ended up filling the void.

I spent a lot of time cruising and realised I knew most of the fruit along the canal banks. As a child, I did a lot of nature walking with my mum, who used to make elderberry and blackberry wines and jams. That came back to me and I decided to make jam as part of the recovery from my accident.

I've always been into food, and I just found it was something I could do. It was also a way to stave off the depression that often goes with long-term health issues. Being outdoors, being creative, and learning a new skill were all really helpful for me. And the connection to the land, very restorative.

There's such a lot of fruit along our inland waterways. I usually pick on the far side of the towpath – fruit that goes to waste. At the time, I couldn't walk very far but I could pick handfuls of plums, cherries and sloes and make a batch of jam. It takes two hours from picking and making to potting, and that was me out for the day. It's very therapeutic. It's not rocket science and at the end I could literally see (or eat) the fruits of my labour.

'Picking fruit along towpaths helped me recover from a head injury'

Family and friends soon started asking me for stuff and it wasn't long before I realised I could make a business out of this. Wild Side Preserves was launched in 2012, followed by a 27-foot engineless boat called *The Jam Butty*, which we tow behind our main narrowboat and sell from at festivals.

Foraging and the business have made my husband and I live much more seasonally than ever before. We are aware of nature in a powerful way and love each season as it approaches (perhaps not so much winter, though that does mean marmalade!) for the excitement of wild food popping up.

For a first-time forager I'd recommend getting hold of a good book. My all-time favourite is *Hedgerow* by John Wright, one of the River Cottage Handbooks. It was my first foraging book and I love it – lots of lovely photos, entertaining anecdotes, and several recipes at the end. It's by no means encyclopaedic but it does cover the dos and don'ts and focuses on easy to identify stuff –perfect for those starting out. ☛ wildsidepreserves.co.uk

FORAGING DOS AND DON'TS

- Never pick anything that you can't identify. If in doubt, leave it.
- Take care not to trample on other plants in the process.
- Only pick what you need and always leave more than you take.
- Give your haul a good wash at home before eating.

WALK ON WATER

It's standing room only for the Hawaiian crossover sport of SUP – or take a punt on something more traditional

6

A long with wild swimming, the breakout star of watersports in the past few years is undoubtedly stand up paddleboarding (SUP). With modern roots in Hawaii's surf scene, it might seem an unlikely import on our staider inland waterways but, just as with swimming, a major lure is its accessibility to all ages and levels of fitness.

SUP is a low-impact exercise, which means you should be able to keep doing it for years and years. But it also gives a full-body workout, so you can feel gratifyingly smug after even a short trip out. It's feted as being particularly good for troublesome bits of your body like knees and backs and, as a non-contact sport (crashing off your board aside), you shouldn't come away from it with any physical injuries.

It can also be a wonderfully sociable activity. Bigger boards can accommodate your partner, pal, child or even the dog, while clubs offer a chance to meet new friends and go out exploring with groups of like-minded people.

No surprise, then, that in May 2021 the Canal & River Trust incorporated paddleboarding into an innovative social prescribing project on the Nottingham & Beeston Canal, along with a designated 'community wellbeing coordinator' to run it. Carol Burrell said the weekly sessions, followed by time socialising afterwards over tea and hot chocolate, were a great opportunity for people to learn new skills, boost their confidence and form new bonds with people they wouldn't normally connect with. As well as developing their paddleboarding technique over the six-week course, participants were encouraged to get over a particularly common phobia with scheduled 'splash sessions'. 'For a lot of people, the fear of falling in was holding them back,' explained Carol, 'and once they had, they quickly realised it wasn't that bad – it's only 4 foot deep and they're not going to die of all the horrible diseases they've read about on the internet.'

A couple of participants enjoyed the experience so much they have come back to support the project as volunteers. For Carol, however, simply raising awareness of the waterways generally is good enough: 'Many people didn't even realise the canal was there, or that they could access it. It's been revelatory to me, too, in that before this project I would never have described myself as a "water person". Seeing all these beautiful spaces has helped with my own wellbeing. It's made me calm, made me appreciate the outdoors more. When you're on the water you're in a different zone, even in the middle of a city you thought you knew well.'

Getting started

Paddleboards can be expensive, so before shelling out make sure you've had a few sessions with an accredited club or instructor, or borrow a friend's board, to make sure you enjoy it and are likely to use it regularly.

On their first go, many people are surprised by the generous size of the board. My introduction to SUP, on a reservoir in the West Midlands, was akin to larking around on something not far off the dimensions of a parish church door. Even more reassuring, the first 15 minutes weren't spent trying to stand at all, just kneeling. This gives you the chance to get a feel for being afloat and how to hold the paddle correctly. (While it might seem counter-intuitive, the best way, FYI, is with the blade angling forward.)

(Above) *Room for a little one? Some boards are big enough to take kids – or even the dog – out for a paddle.*

(Left) *A group of paddleboarders at Thorpe St Andrew in Norfolk.*

From prayer pose, the transition to 'upright and grinning madly' is gratifyingly swift. Much like an accelerated March of Progress, I was encouraged to adopt an ape-like hunch on all fours before wobbling my way up. Then it's time to work on your stroke; ideally, reaching forward with your back straight and knees slightly bent, pushing the paddle down with a digging motion and, once the blade is fully submerged, bringing it back level with your heel and out again. After three or four strokes, simply move your paddle to the other side of the board, swap your hands around too and hey, look, you're paddling!

1 Holding the board by its edges, work yourself onto it and adopt a kneeling position just behind the centre.

2 One foot at a time, slowly move into a squatting position, keeping your hands on the board to stabilise it.

3 Have your feet roughly shoulder-width apart and turn your heels inward slightly.

4 You don't have to stand up in one motion. Start by raising your chest and keep your knees bent. Once you're balanced and your chest is vertical, stand up fully by extending your legs.

5 Time to look at your hands. You'll need to position one over the T-shaped handle of your paddle, while the other hand (closest to the side you're paddling on) is halfway down the shaft. Gently start paddling.

Equipment and costs

As well as settling your budget before you start shopping for boards, it's a good idea to pin down whether you want an inflatable or rigid one. The former has the advantage of being slightly cheaper (depending on quality), less easily damaged, lighter, and easier to store and transport. They're also, perhaps crucially, less painful to land on, so ideal for beginners.

For a mid-range board, expect to pay in the region of £400–£600. You'll also need to add the cost of a paddle on to this, plus a pump if you're going down the inflatable road. Many deals include all three, which could be more cost effective. As could scouring the internet for second-hand equipment.

On the back of your board should be a leash with a Velcro band to attach to your ankle. Use it. Not only will it stop you losing your board if you tip into the drink, it means you're always linked to a pretty handy piece of life-saving paraphernalia – the buoyant board itself.

Depending on the weather and water temperature, you may also want to wear a wetsuit. If you're a beginner, or paddling on a stretch of water that demands you wear one, a personal flotation device should also be on your kit list.

The final thing you might need to fork out on is a licence. The Canal & River Trust, Scottish Canals, the Environment Agency and Broads Authority all require you to have one for paddling on their patch. You can purchase annual or short visit permits from their websites. Alternatively, you can buy an annual licence from £45 as part of membership of British Canoeing.

● *Make sure you've got a licence from the relevant navigation authority to paddle on their waters.*

WALK ON WATER

BEST SUP SPOTS FOR NEW STARTERS

Beautiful Bala

Set in Snowdonia National Park, Bala Lake (Llyn Tegid) boasts
deep, clear water, stunning mountain scenery and some
excellent wildlife-spotting opportunities (from otters to red
kites and buzzards). In summer, the lake can get particularly
busy with boats and canoes. Time your visit carefully, and
make sure you get a lake permit from the Pay and Display
machines at Llyn Tegid's foreshore car park before setting off
(snowdonia.gov.wales/visit/llyn-tegid/llyn-tegid-watersports-
permits/). If you're looking to hire a board, Bala Watersports
(www.balawatersports.com) will be able to kit you out.

Bright lights of Greater Manchester

Tantalising glimpses of suburbia and hangovers of an industrial past can be
just as thrilling to a paddleboarder as postcard-pretty rural stretches. The
Bridgewater Canal offers this in spades. It was built by the Duke of Bridgewater

to transport coal from his mines at Worsley,
across the stone arches of Barton Aqueduct
and into Manchester, and officially opened
in 1761.

Paddleboarding is a relative newcomer
on this navigation, having only been
permitted since 2021. This followed a survey
in 2020 by the Bridgewater Canal Company
into the health and wellbeing benefits of
the canal during Covid-19 lockdowns, and
SUP was a popular request for additional
recreational activities on the waterway. Out
of 335 people surveyed, 284 said using the canal had positively impacted their
mental health and wellbeing by an average of 84 per cent. More than 40 per cent
also said the canal made them feel either 'relaxed' or 'happy'.

Go super-sized in Scotland

The Cairngorms isn't just Britain's largest national park, it's also home to some
jumbo paddleboards. Head to Loch Insh Outdoor Centre with a crowd, and you'll
find four adults (or seven kids) can fit on to a 'double' board for a
sociable, albeit squeezed, tour of this beautiful stretch of water.

The centre, based 11 km (7 miles) south of Aviemore, also
offers an 8am sunrise trip for SUP devotees. According to the
blurb this is the best time to experience the lake, when it is
shrouded in ethereal early mist.

(Top) Lake Bala is the largest natural lake in Wales.

(Centre) The Bridgewater Canal in Manchester.

*(Bottom) Trees and mist-shrouded hills are reflected in
the calm waters of Loch Insh.*

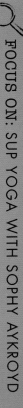

FOCUS ON: SUP YOGA WITH SOPHY AYKROYD

Mastered standing up on your board? How about a series of sun salutations next? Sophy Aykroyd, an instructor with Active360 on the Thames and Grand Union Canal in London, explains why more and more people are giving SUP yoga (and Pilates) a go.

What is SUP yoga?
Put simply, it's when you take a traditional yoga class on to the water and the paddleboard becomes your new floating yoga mat.

Isn't that tricky on a river?
We choose our locations carefully, avoid tides and use anchors to keep the boards in place. You just clip your board on to a rope with a carabiner or bungee, so you're not going to be floating off anywhere…

Can you take part in SUP yoga as a total beginner in both paddleboarding and yoga?
Totally, because we use such lovely big boards (81–86cm/32–34in wide), which provide a comfortable and stable platform. I start very much with kneeling or seated or lying poses. Of course, if you've done paddleboarding you're going to find it easier, but it's not a prerequisite. If I've got complete novices in the session I usually take them for a little paddle first, so they get used to the board and buoyancy. By the time they've anchored, they're usually not as nervous. People's main concern is falling in, but in our SUP yoga and Pilates sessions (as opposed to general paddleboarding on the river) that doesn't tend to happen as you're tied up and not tackling tidal waters.

How long do the sessions last?
About an hour. People usually come off the boards at the end feeling exhilarated, and that they've really achieved something out of the ordinary. The yoga itself is more challenging than in a studio because you've got the instability to factor in. By being exposed to the elements and having to adjust to the movement of the water, you maximise your

☞ continued on page 84

83

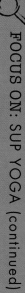

☞ continued from page 83

FOCUS ON: SUP YOGA (continued)

core stability throughout the entire class.

There are mental health benefits too. People very much have to concentrate on what they're doing and where their limbs are going. You really have to focus, and so it takes you away from the stresses of everyday life. Plus there are all the associated benefits of being outside and close to nature.

How close to nature do you come?

On one of my ordinary SUP sessions, when I was out on the Thames with a mother and her son, we were actually boarded by a seal! He was well known on the stretch between Kew and Richmond, and we even had a name for him – Freddie Mercury. But having him jump on the mother's board first, and then the son's, was something else. It was amazing.

☞ active360.co.uk
Prices vary depending on the duration of the class, but start at £25 per person for a 1-hour group session. SUP yoga and Pilates can be practised wearing your usual fitness clothing, but wetsuits are available on request if you prefer. People who are not entirely comfortable on water can also wear buoyancy aids.

The (mostly) genteel sport of punting

'Like Bank Holiday at Margate, with gramophones and bathing-dresses and everybody barging into everybody else.' Thus does crime writer Dorothy L Sayers describe the punting scene on the River Cherwell in Oxford in her 1935 novel *Gaudy Night*. Nearly 90 years on, the university city is still choked with punt traffic come summer, even if the gramophones have been replaced by Spotify playlists tinnily thrumming from smartphones.

While Oxford and Cambridge have the monopoly on punting, it was in fact the River Thames that spawned it as both a fiercely competitive sport and an idle pastime. Pictures of regattas from the 1860s through to the 1950s show huge numbers of punts filled with spectators. Sadly, they are now something of a rarity, even at Henley,

and seldom seen outside of the context of the Oxbridge tourist trade.

BOATS AND TECHNIQUE

Punts are recognisable for their flat bottom (useful in shallow waters) and square-cut bow and stern, making them very stable and relatively easy to manoeuvre in either direction.

You will generally find a choice of two kinds of punts to hire. Single-width boats are rented by the hour, usually to absolute novices to zigzag around in, while double-width boats have 'professional' chauffeurs who make it all look a lot easier and will likely also keep you entertained with a running commentary about all the historic university buildings you pass.

Perhaps the best way to learn is by example – starting out in a boat with a competent punter and scrutinising their every move. After that, graduate to hands-on practice and try different rivers, or vary which stretches you tackle along the same one.

In terms of where to position yourself to punt, stand near the back of the craft and as near to the side as you dare. To get moving, you push against the riverbed with a 3.6–4.8-metre (12–16-foot) pole, fitted, at the bottom, with a metal 'shoe'. The technique is, loosely, a case of 'throwing' the pole down close to the side of the punt and guiding it with the lower hand.

When it touches the bottom, reach forward with both hands and gently push the pole past your chest. 'Gently' really is the operative word – you're less likely to steer wildly.

At the end of the stroke, simply let the pole float up like a rudder behind you and, when the punt is going straight, bring up the pole hand over hand until you can throw it down again. And so starts the next stroke.

A punt jam by Magdalen Bridge in Oxford in springtime.

COMPETITIVE PUNTING

Punts were originally built as platforms for Thames fishermen and watermen, says Peter Williams of Dittons Skiff and Punting Club. 'These craft were heavy wooden things and required huge skill and stamina to propel. Vying to get passengers aboard or to find the best fishing spot spawned a competitive strand to punting, with wealthy patrons soon putting up big prizes.'

By 1885 this emerging sport was codified under a set of rules by the newly formed Thames Punting Club (TPC), and the early craft were soon replaced by narrower and lighter ones optimised for speed. The TPC introduced standardised 'regulation' punts towards the end of the 1800s to ensure fairness.

These days, punt racing struggles to garner the attention it deserves, but there remain ten regattas a year, including the annual championships on the Bray Reach at Maidenhead every August. There has recently been some

Competitors take part in the Thames Punting Championships at Staines in 1938.

evidence of renewed interest in the sport as people increasingly recognise its mental and physical health benefits.

However, capitalising on this is not going to be easy, not least because there are fewer boatbuilders with the necessary skills to build the craft. What's more, river conditions make punting on the Thames trickier than it was 140 years ago, says Peter. 'Punters are being forced further out into the stream by overgrown banks, where they are vulnerable to the wash from motorboats. Propellers are also damaging the gravel riverbeds, the firmness of which punters need.'

Don't write off Thames punting just yet though. Its elegance and gentle reminder of a lost 'golden age' on the river give it continued cachet, and the remaining Thames clubs welcome new members and offer coaching.

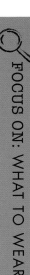

FOCUS ON: WHAT TO WEAR

Cambridge punting favourite Scudamore's (scudamores.com), which hires boats as well as offering chauffeured trips, has some excellent fashion advice on an 'adventure checklist' blog post, including rubber-soled footwear for maximum grip ('and minimum embarrassment'). It also politely advises avoiding clothes made of thin, flowing fabrics, which can attain 'degrees of transparency' when wet. Continuing on a public decency theme, skirts and dresses are a no-no too, unless paired with leggings: 'Everything to do with punting and getting in and out of boats has got knicker-flashing embarrassment written all over it.'

But I refer you back to Dorothy L Sayers for the last word on the traditional punting wardrobe, as her *Gaudy Night* heroine Harriet Vane elucidates:

"The Punting Girl."

● *Postcard of 'The Punting Girl' from The Sports Girls series by James Henderson, circa 1905.*

Harriet smiled to herself as she went to change for the river. If Peter was keen on keeping up decayed traditions he would find plenty of opportunity by keeping to a pre-War standard of watermanship, manners and dress. Especially dress. A pair of grubby shorts or a faded regulation suit rolled negligently about the waist was the modern version of Cherwell fashions for men; for women, a sun-bathing costume with (for the tender-footed) a pair of gaily-coloured beach sandals.

Harriet shook her head at the sunshine, which was now hot as well as bright. Even for the sake of startling Peter, she was not prepared to offer a display of grilled back and mosquito-bitten legs. She would go seemly and comfortable.

The Dean, meeting her under the beeches, gazed with exaggerated surprise at her dazzling display of white linen and pipe-clay.

'If this were twenty years ago I should say you were going on the river.'

'I am. Hand in hand with a statelier past.'

THE OXFORD END V. THE CAMBRIDGE END

Pleasure punting arrived in Oxford and Cambridge at the start of the 20th century and both cities still embrace it. There is one marked difference, however, in how punting developed between the two places and it's all down to where the punter stands. In Oxford, expect to be at the stern, and proceeding bow first. In Cambridge, the punter instead stands on the flat raised bow or deck (a less stable practice) and propels the boat stern first. Why the riskier option on the Cam? Allegedly because in Edwardian times the lady undergraduates of Girton College felt it better showed off their ankles.

Top tips to enjoy punting

AVOID THE TOURISTS

Bear in mind that the popularity of punting beside the old colleges in Cambridge, especially, produces bottlenecks – and frequent collisions – on the section known as The Backs. A more tranquil, and no less lovely, trip is heading out of town towards the village of Grantchester. Another option is to start early or go last thing in the evening. At the very least, avoid peak tourist time: generally between about 1pm and 5pm on Saturday afternoon.

BOOK AHEAD

Don't expect to be able to hop straight on a boat, especially in summer or if you're going on a shared punt tour. If you haven't booked in advance you might find there isn't much availability at all during busy times.

BE PREPARED TO GET WET

If you're not the punter, there's probably not much risk of you falling in. To be on the safe side, though, and certainly if you're the one holding the pole, keep valuables like mobile phones and cameras out of your pockets and safely stowed somewhere inside the craft. Remember, too, how unpredictable British summers can be and pack an umbrella for peace of mind.

Punting in Cambridge.

FLYBOARDING INTO THE FUTURE

For Frenchman Franky Zapata, walking on water is all just a bit, well, *passé*. The next big thing in watersports, according to the pioneer of the personal jetpack, is levitating over it. Zapata unveiled his so-called flyboard in 2012, and has since developed the technology to perform a record-breaking Channel crossing in 22 minutes, with a refuelling stop at midpoint.

Adrenaline junkies can give it a go in a handful of locations across the UK, including London Docklands and Dumfries. Essentially, it involves standing on a board connected by a long hose to a watercraft. Water is forced under pressure to jet nozzles under the participant's feet, which provide enough thrust to 'fly' 6 metres (20 feet) clear of the surface.

Franky Zapata tests his invention, the Zapata Flyboard, in 2012.

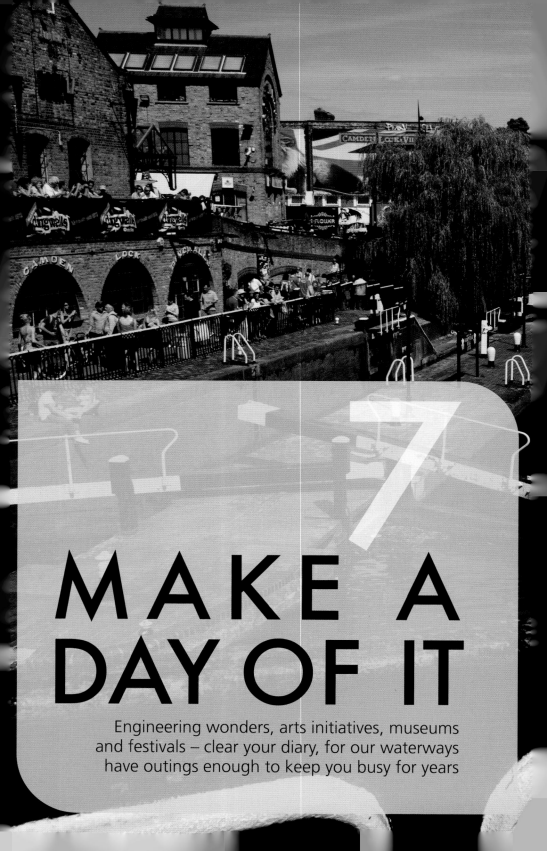

MAKE A DAY OF IT

Engineering wonders, arts initiatives, museums and festivals – clear your diary, for our waterways have outings enough to keep you busy for years

I n 1946, as the Inland Waterways Association kicked off its campaign for the conservation, use, maintenance and restoration of Britain's threatened canal network, the charity's co-founder, Robert Aickman, had something of a marketing brainwave. As a way of highlighting the jewels in our waterways' crown, and bringing to public attention those that were threatened with dereliction, he riffed on the Seven Wonders of the Ancient World idea to come up with a list of awe-inspiring sights specific to our inland navigation system, and all are still well worthy of a visit.

'Awe' – with its associated goosebumps and slack jaws – is a strange sort of emotion. Spotlighted by the Romantics and puzzled over by scientists ever since, recent efforts to quantify the effect it has on people include a joint study by the University of California and Trinity College, Dublin that focused on the emotional benefits of so-called 'awe walks' in older adults. As part of the research, 60 people took weekly 15-minute walks for eight weeks. Participants were randomly assigned either to a group that oriented them to experience wonder during their stroll or to a control walk group. All were tasked with taking photographs of themselves during the walks and rating their emotional experience. The results, published in 2021 in the journal *Emotion*, found the 'awe walkers' reported

● The Anderton Boat Lift in Cheshire connects the River Weaver and Trent & Mersey Canal.

reduced stress, increased creativity and sociability, as well as greater humility and generosity. This was reflected in the selfies they took, which showed a growing focus on their surroundings rather than themselves, plus measurably broader smiles by the end of the study.

There are plenty of places to find awe on our inland waterways, but Aickman's list, which showcases waterways engineering at its most ambitious, is a great place to start. In most instances there's enough going on at the site or in the immediate vicinity to make a whole day of it.

THE SEVEN WONDERS OF THE WATERWAYS
(Plus one extra)

1 Anderton Boat Lift

(*Left*) The Canal & River Trust likens this imposing boat lift in Northwich, Cheshire to a 'giant, three-storey-high iron spider'. It may appear the stuff of science fiction, but its design is all about functionality – namely, to lift boats 15 metres (50 feet) from the River Weaver to the Trent & Mersey Canal in two huge water tanks. Opened in 1875, it was initially steam powered before being converted to electric operation in 1908. Boats can still hop between the two waterways, and there's a glass-sided trip-boat running from April to the end of October for people who don't have their own craft. Passengers will not only experience the lift itself, but also enjoy a brief chug along the scenic Weaver Navigation as part of the 60-minute trip. You can find out even more about the lift in a behind-the-scenes tour, which starts in the visitor centre before heading out on a guided walk along the aqueduct to the control room and machine deck and finally climbing to the very top of the structure.
☛ canalrivertrust.org.uk/places-to-visit/anderton-boat-lift-visitor-centre

2 Barton Swing Aqueduct

(*Right*) Built in the 1890s to carry the Bridgewater Canal over the Manchester Ship Canal at Barton upon Irwell, Greater Manchester, this fantastic piece of Victorian engineering still works: the aqueduct (essentially an iron trough 72 metres/235 feet long) uses guillotine

gates to seal off water at both ends before pivoting on an island in the middle of the ship canal. If you're lucky, you'll time your visit to see it slowly swing open. The nearby Barton Road swing bridge is of a similar design and controlled from the same tower.

3 Bingley Five Rise Locks

(*Right*) The first of two lock flights on Aickman's list, this one is located at Bingley in Yorkshire and boasts being the steepest staircase flight (where the lower gate of one lock forms the upper gate of the next) in the country. It raises the level of the Leeds & Liverpool Canal by 18 metres (60 feet) over a distance of around 97 metres (320 feet). The locks were built in 1774 and have remained relatively unchanged since – but not unchallenged. Leicestershire's Foxton Locks opened little over 30 years later and, with an impressive ten-lock staircase, are just as worth a visit.
☛ canalrivertrust.org.uk/places-to-visit/Bingley

● *Historic Barton Swing Aqueduct still carries canal boats over the Manchester Ship Canal.*

4 Burnley Embankment

(*Below*) Staying on the Leeds & Liverpool Canal, head over to Burnley for the largest canal embankment in Britain at almost a mile long and 18 metres (60 feet) high. It carries the waterway across the River Calder and its tributary, the Brun, providing a wonderful panorama of Burnley's industrial surrounds as it does so. While you're admiring the view, spare a thought for the people charged with constructing the embankment. The project utilised half a million tons of earth displaced by construction of a nearby canal cutting and tunnel, and moved to the site by horse and cart. It finally opened, after four years of blood, sweat, tears and no small cost, in 1801.

5 Caen Hill Locks

(*Below*) More locks – 29 of them this time, on the Kennet & Avon Canal in Devizes, Wiltshire. They are packed into just over 3km (2 miles), although it's the main section of 16 locks, designated a scheduled ancient monument, that most people come to see and photograph. If you've got an energetic crew, boats can clear this section in two hours, while the full run can take up to six hours. A nearby café and pub provide welcome restoratives after (and during...) the slog.
☛ canalrivertrust.org.uk/places-to-visit/caen-hill-locks

6 Standedge Tunnel

(*Left*) This is Britain's longest (and deepest) canal tunnel, and was only reopened to boat traffic in 2001 after being unused for more than half a century. Located on the Huddersfield Narrow Canal near Marsden, you can spook yourself in the 5.6km (3½ miles) of sub-Pennine darkness by hopping aboard a 30-minute 'discovery' boat ride (£8pp), or go all the way through to Diggle for £35pp. There's also a dog-friendly café at the Marsden end, plus an interesting visitor centre that tells the story of the tunnel, from its planning and 17-year construction to its mixed fortunes in the two centuries since.
☛ canalrivertrust.org.uk/places-to-visit/standedge-tunnel-and-visitor-centre

7 Pontcysyllte Aqueduct

(*Above*) Thomas Telford's record-breaking aqueduct carrying the Llangollen Canal over the River Dee offers probably the biggest thrill of them all. Measuring 305 metres (1,000 feet) long, its highest point is 38.4 metres (126 feet) above the valley, which it spans in 19 elegant arches. You can walk across the aqueduct for free, or find a space aboard a trip-boat. Either way you'll want your camera to hand, for the views are sublime. There's more information about the structure at Trevor Basin Visitor Centre, and a couple of places to grab a bite to eat. For those wishing to prolong their visit, pontcysyllte-aqueduct.co.uk has ideas for other heritage structures and beauty spots along this stretch of canal, 17.7km (11 miles) of which have been designated a UNESCO World Heritage Site.

☛ canalrivertrust.org.uk/places-to-visit/pontcysyllte-aqueduct-world-heritage-site

8 Falkirk Wheel

(*Below*) Built long after Aickman compiled his original list, this rotating boat lift – the only one of its kind in the world – is a worthy addition to the seven wonders already detailed. Connecting the Forth and Clyde Canal with the Union Canal for the first time since the 1930s, it opened in 2002 as part of the Millennium Link project to regenerate central Scotland's canals and reconnect Glasgow with Edinburgh. Planners could have simply recreated the historic lock flight once located here, but instead chose to build a real showstopper of a lift, which raises boats by 24 metres (79 feet). The lift itself stands 35 metres (115 feet) high (roughly the size of eight double-decker buses), and can carry up to eight boats at a time. There's a visitor centre, which is free to peruse, as well as a shop and café. Hour-long boat trips depart from the front of the visitor centre and include passage along the aqueduct to the Union Canal and back. There are also footpaths from the Falkirk Wheel to Rough Castle Roman Fort, which has one of the best-preserved stretches of the Antonine Wall.

☛ www.scottishcanals.co.uk/falkirk-wheel

Be a culture vulture

As well as offering plenty to marvel at, days out along our inland waterways can provide a hit of culture, tapping into something that used to be a key part of the 'waterways wellness' scene of antiquity. Take the Romans, for example, whose luxurious bathing complexes – called *thermae* – did not just offer plunge pools, saunas and heated bathing water, but also lecture halls, libraries, rooms for poetry readings, and places to buy and eat food.

The modern equivalent doesn't exist in spa culture as we know it today, but still finds echoes in the growing number of festivals, floating shops, galleries, theatres, and other arts and community initiatives on or along our rivers and canals. Like the Romans, we're getting better at linking the concept of 'taking the waters' to vital social, artistic, cultural and creative endeavours, and so widening the scope of a waterways wellness escape.

The Canal & River Trust, which looks after the majority of navigable waterways in England and Wales, has been particularly good at this. When the charity launched in 2012, for example, it immediately partnered with Arts Council England on a project called Locklines to carve and inlay poetry into certain lock gates around the system. At the time, CRT's arts development manager, Tim Eastop, reiterated the 'longstanding link between arts and the waterways', while Jo Bell, one of the poets whose lines were used for the initiative, identified how our canals have changed from merely trunk roads to something more cerebral: 'Places to think, or to stop ourselves thinking.'

Today there are all sorts of ways to sample these cultural offerings, which often reflect the varied communities our waterways pass through. The suggestions that follow are largely focused on long-term projects or permanent sites, but keep your eyes peeled for smaller, one-off or temporary initiatives specific to your local canal, lake, river or reservoir.

Festivals and floating markets

Bristol Harbour Festival celebrates the city's waterways heritage with family-friendly activities along the water's edge, Tall Ships and a host of visiting boats all decorated for the occasion.

Let's start with the canals, which offer a glut of summer festivals and floating markets. The most famous is probably London's **Canalway Cavalcade** at Little Venice, where cheerfully decorated boats jostle for attention between live music, market stalls, food and drink, children's activities, Morris dancers, competitions and parades. Among the most popular elements is the legendary procession of illuminated boats.

Just as lively is **Rickmansworth Canal Festival**, which usually attracts over 100 boats from across the country and occupies part of the Aquadrome and the Grand Union Canal towpath between Stockers Lock and Batchworth Lock. **Middlewich Folk and Boat Festival** is another favourite on the circuit. It has provided family attractions and musical entertainment for over 30 years, as well as showcasing Middlewich's rich canal history with a colourful flotilla of narrowboats on the Trent & Mersey Canal below Big Lock or above Kings Lock, and on the Shropshire Union Canal above Wardle.

On our rivers, look out especially for **Totally Thames Festival**, a month-long season of physical and digital events every September, which serve as a celebration of the River Thames in London. Meanwhile, **Bristol Harbour Festival**, now past its 50th year, is a flagship event for the city's unrivalled arts and culture sector, with a programme of more than 300 artists and performers, along with 200 visiting boats. Bristol has hosted the festival since 1971, when it was launched as part of a campaign (ultimately successful) to save the city's docks from being filled in.

If you want to ogle heritage boats specifically, the **Thames Traditional Boat Festival**, **Braunston Historic**

Boat Rally and Gloucester Tall Ships Festival are the ones to head for. The latter is a biannual event and allows maritime enthusiasts to climb aboard some of the visiting boats, speak to their captains and discover more about the history of these glorious vessels, as well as enjoying live entertainment throughout the weekend.

Most canal and river festivals welcome roving traders to exhibit as part of a **floating market**, selling everything from cakes and crafts to ironwork and vinyl records. Separate trading events take place across the country throughout the year, with a list of upcoming ones on the Roving Canal Traders Association website: rcta.org.uk.

If you're in the market to buy a boat, visit the **Crick Boat Show** at Crick Marina on the Leicester Line of the Grand Union Canal near Daventry. Now Britain's biggest inland waterways festival, it offers a huge pop-up chandlery, free boat trips, seminars for both first-time buyers and seasoned helmsmen alike, and, crucially, over 50 craft to look around. You can vote for the one that impresses you most over the weekend as part of the now traditional Favourite Boat in Show award.

Finally, a growing number of music festivals let the bands and DJs share top billing with some beautiful waterscapes. For dance music, head to the **Riverside Festival Glasgow** on the banks of the Clyde. It's credited as Scotland's premier electronic music festival and the iconic location in the grounds of the Riverside Museum doesn't do its reputation any harm. Meanwhile, **Wilderness Festival** in Oxfordshire's idyllic Cornbury Park marries many of the aspects of a traditional music festival with wellbeing activities like wild swimming in the lake and a waterside spa.

● (Top) *Canalway Cavalcade in London's Little Venice.*

(Centre) *The Puppet Barge.*

(Left) *A lakeside spa at Wilderness Festival.*

Take in a show

Puppet shows have been a staple of the seaside since Victorian times, but there's also a 40-odd year tradition of it on our inland waterways – at least in London. The red-and-yellow canvas-covered **Puppet Barge** is based in Little Venice and operates from a 22-metre (72-foot) former working boat. Shows typically last 30 minutes each half with an interval in between, and the high quality of the performances have won the company legions of fans, including Brad Pitt and Angelina Jolie. With a 55-member audience capacity, the company is disappointed if it doesn't sell out these days so book well in advance.

As well as theatre, London has seen several iterations of **floating cinema** in recent years, including a dedicated cinema boat plying its canals, plus pop-up screenings of classic movies as part of a series of sunset Thames cruises organised by *Time Out*. Keep your eyes peeled, in particular, for the return of an initiative that first launched during lockdown on the Regent's Canal (www.openaire.co.uk). It saw film buffs pile in to 16 electric GoBoats and enjoy a quick zip around the water before mooring up at Merchant Square, Paddington, to don headphones and watch a blockbuster, cult classic or musical on a giant 6x3-metre hi-res LED video screen. Snacks and street food were available to order direct to the boats.

If you can't make it to the capital, let our waterways arts initiatives come to you. **Mikron** (www.mikron.org.uk) claims to be the UK's most prolific theatre company, touring to over 120 venues per year on its narrowboat, *Tyseley*, in the summer, and by road in spring and autumn. In 2022 it celebrated its 50th anniversary, and estimates that in this time it has written 66 original shows, composed and written 396 songs, issued over 240 actor musician contracts, performed over 5,200 times to over 436,000 people and spent 34,000 boating hours on the inland waterways. Quirky performance venues have included dry docks, allotments, rallies, restaurants and even a tunnel.

Rather more recent, but still itinerant, is the UK's only **floating mobile public library**, which launched in 2021. It's based on an eye-catching narrowboat called RV *Furor Scribendi* (meaning 'furious writing') and has an exclusive focus on short-story collections, including many non-English language books. The boat can hold up to 1,000 books and also accommodates reading and writing residencies for professionals, amateurs and complete novices.

Heritage happiness

Our canals are home to over 2,700 listed structures, 50 scheduled ancient monuments and five UNESCO World Heritage Sites. According to the Canal & River Trust, a 20-minute towpath walk alone will take in a handful of more interesting heritage items, from milestones and lock gates to bridges and toll houses. What relevance does this have to anyone who's not a history buff? Well, according to research from Historic England's Heritage and Society report in 2019, 'heritage counts' no matter who we are. It connects us to the world around as well as engaging us in our past. As such, it can be a mine of wellbeing benefits, fostering a sense of belonging and boosting confidence and general happiness.

While the Wonders of the Waterways detailed earlier in this chapter can provide an obvious heritage fix, there are plenty of smaller-scale or less well-known sites, especially in the industrial heartland of the canal network, the Midlands. In Dudley, for example, which lays claim to the second-longest navigable canal tunnel in the UK, you can have a go at 'legging' through, as the working boatmen did of yore, aboard a **Dudley Canal & Tunnel Trust** trip-boat (dudleycanaltrust.org.uk/). Alternatively, head up to the Trent & Mersey Canal at **Middleport, Stoke-on-Trent** (www.burleigh.co.uk/pages/ visit-middleport-pottery), to find out how our waterways helped create its world-famous potteries industry. You can take a factory tour, wander around the visitor centre and Burleigh factory shop, or simply imbibe the history over a cuppa and something to eat at the canal-side café, based in the original packing house.

Finally, don't forget Britain's wealth of superb waterways museums. **Windermere Jetty Museum** of Boats, Steam and Stories (lakelandarts.org. uk/windermere-jetty-museum/) should be top of the list, having only opened its doors in 2019 following a £20m development of the site of the former Windermere Steamboat Museum. Located north of the village of Bowness, it looks, on first glance, little more than a cluster of barns close to the water's edge. Get closer and explore inside, however, and you'll understand why it was shortlisted for the Stirling Prize and branded 'the most beautiful boat shed in Britain' by *The Times*. Its spectacular design more than does justice to the vessels inside, which range from the sublime (1896-built *Branksome*, the finest example of a Victorian steam launch and the flagship of the collection with its walnut panelling and velvet upholstery), to the altogether more humble (Beatrix Potter's rowing boat, knocked together out of old floorboards). For the ultimate experience on Windermere, you can even enjoy a cruise on a restored heritage boat from the museum's collection. Kids may also like the delightful Model Boating Pond, where they can sail their mini boats for free.

Elsewhere, you're spoilt for choice when it comes to canal history. Choose from the **National Waterways Museums at Ellesmere Port and Gloucester** (canalrivertrust.org.uk/ places-to-visit/national-waterways-museum), the **London Canal Museum** in King's Cross (www.canalmuseum.org. uk), or **Stoke Bruerne**'s offering on the Grand Union Canal just south of the Blisworth Tunnel in Northamptonshire

(canalrivertrust.org.uk/places-to-visit/ stoke-bruerne/visit-the-canal-museum). In Scotland, the canal museum at **Linlithgow Canal Centre** (www.lucs. org.uk) is housed in a former canal stable and describes the origin, decline and renaissance of the Edinburgh and Glasgow Union Canal. Boat models, original tools and equipment, and objects from the working life of the canal are also on show.

Get up close to motorboats, steam launches, *sailing yachts and record-breaking speed boats at* *the excellent Windermere Jetty Museum.*

PICK YOUR WATERWAYS TOWN 'TRIBE'

Everyone has their favourite waterways town for a day out. Rowers will pilgrimage to Henley, while Braunston offers a spiritual home-on-land to anyone with working-boat heritage on the canals. For foreign tourists, Windermere is the quintessential English lakeside retreat, while across the border, Loch Linnhe's Fort William is a firm favourite among Highland walkers, Great Glen-goers, and Harry Potter fans (looking to hop aboard the Jacobite steam train) alike.

I'm prepared to nail my own colours to the mast and declare the World Heritage Site of **Saltaire** (saltairevillage.info/) *(Right),* on the Leeds & Liverpool Canal and River Aire in Yorkshire, the best waterside town for a day trip – and it has the 'wellness' of inhabitants at its very heart. Its creator, a textile tycoon turned Victorian do-gooder called Titus Salt, was so moved by the squalid living and working conditions of local mill staff that he snapped up a tract of land 5km (3 miles) from Bradford and set his heart on building something altogether more ambrosial for them.

The model village opened in 1853 and its centrepiece, Salts Mill, became known as 'The Palace of Industry' – a place where Puritan hard graft meets the sublime. These days it houses a David Hockney gallery and simply marvellous bookshop.

Approaching by boat, you're flanked not just by this imposing building, but by the 'New Mill' opposite as well. When the sun comes out, a perfect reflection doubles their size. Draw closer and you're effectively blinkered by the buildings – nothing but a ribbon of sky and water getting a look in between those vertiginous honey walls. The effect isn't exactly claustrophobic, but something even more breathtaking – as if a curtain has been pulled on the 21st century, and you're back in the working heyday of the waterways. That is, a sanitised, celestial working heyday, because all is warm-coloured, Italianate and subversively beautiful.

Salts Mill from the River Aire, Saltaire.

8 ROW YOUR BOAT

Row, scull or paddle – there are lots of ways to go gently (and a little more roughly) down the stream

Although rowing is lumped in with all the other 'sitting down sports' us Brits are supposed to be genetically good at, I don't think any of us are wholly convinced that being excellently sedentary in front of, say, Netflix for three hours a night is necessarily a shoo-in to the sort of success Steve Redgrave or Katherine Grainger have achieved on their backsides.

The thing about those sorts is their obvious superhumanness. Even on their bums in the boat, they still seem to tower above most sub-6-foot mortals. And then there's the mental strength needed for those early morning river sessions and gruelling stints on the rowing machines.

Finally: the Posh Thing. Rowing still hasn't quite shaken off its reputation for being all blazers and public school boys and going on the lash at Henley.

And so a lot of us simply don't bother.

And that's a shame, because the sport is making huge efforts to encourage more diverse participation, and the benefits are myriad. For starters, consider the physical workout it gives you. Rowing can burn up to 600 calories per hour, improve cardio-respiratory fitness and give full-body conditioning. But it has also, over all my years writing and reading about the waterways, provided some of the most inspiring stories of positive change. Fulham Reach Boat Club, for example, is using rowing to rehabilitate young offenders as part of its 'Boats Not Bars' scheme. The club's founder, Steve O'Connor, says the grit and psychological toughness required to succeed at the sport uniquely taps into some prisoners' mentality. Or consider the story of Xander Van Der Poll, a student paralysed from the waist down after falling from a tree aged 19, who took up rowing as part of his recovery and now hopes to embark on a Paralympic rowing career. In a video for British Rowing he said the attraction of the sport was that water is a great leveller. Able-bodied or not, everyone is just trying to make their boat go as fast as it can, he explained.

On top of this, rowing as part of a squad requires trust, commitment and excellent communication skills. In other words, not only will you get into shape physically and mentally, but also improve teamwork skills to build friendships for life.

IT'S ALL IN THE LEGS

Rowing might look like an upper-body sport, but it's your legs that will get the biggest workout on the water. At the catch – when the oar goes into the water – your legs provide the drive, and the arms and back then finish the stroke.

No clue to club member

British Rowing's website (britishrowing. org) is a great resource to plunder for information about getting started in the sport, whatever your age. Indeed, British Rowing is keen to stress that rowing is not the preserve of the super-fit university student, with good numbers of over-50s signing up as novices and some people still competing into their 80s.

The website offers advice on technique and training, or you can search for local rowing clubs by postcode and sign up for a Learn to Row course. This will cost between £90 and £120 and usually last six weeks, with one 2-hour session per week (although the exact time commitment may differ from club to club). Alternatively, look for clubs that offer free taster sessions.

If you like the experience, you may be persuaded to join the club, fees for which will depend on the level you want to row at. There are often special rates for young people, pensioners and social members, and the obvious advantage is you won't have to fork out on buying your own boat. You don't need any special kit to start with either.

There are also a number of clubs offering adaptive rowing for those looking to enter the sport with a disability. According to British Rowing, a greater number of accessible rowing venues plus advances in specialist equipment mean that rowing is becoming 'a leader in inclusive sport'.

Its website has a useful FAQ section (www.britishrowing.org/go-rowing/learn-to-row/adaptive-rowing/adaptive-rowing-faqs/) with advice, for example,

ONE OAR OR TWO?

The term 'rowing' refers to the use of a single oar grasped in both hands (also known as 'sweep rowing'), while 'sculling' involves the use of two oars, one in each hand.

on how to row if you have limited hand function (answer: self-closing Velcro gloves that tension to wrap fingers around the oar/scull handle and are suitable for disabilities as diverse as cerebral palsy, stroke recovery and finger amputations), plus how a rower can keep in time in a crew if they have a visual impairment.

● (Inset) *The sport is making efforts to entice a broader range of ages, from kids to retirees.*

(Below) *Joining a rowing club can help you progress within the sport and means you won't have to fork out on your own boat.*

Spectator sport

If you don't fancy competing or training but still want to be involved in rowing, then coaching or volunteering at club events could be a great alternative. Rowing tours (whether at home or abroad) are also a popular way to stay involved.

Alternatively, turn up as a spectator to your local regatta or watch the top-level stuff on the Thames. Oxford and Cambridge universities' annual **Boat Race** (www.theboatrace.org/) is a relatively easy one to view, covering a 6.7 km (4.2-mile) stretch of the river from Putney to Mortlake in London. You can find places to watch on either side of the river along the full length of the course, but some of the best spots include Putney Bridge, Putney Embankment and Bishop's Park (at the start), Craven Cottage (for the first mile), Hammersmith and Barnes (mid-course), and Dukes Meadows and Chiswick Bridge (for the finish).

Henley Royal Regatta (www.hrr.co.uk/) requires a bit more forward planning. Since the Regatta owns most of the riverbank and parking area on the Oxfordshire side and some of it on the opposite Buckinghamshire side, you really do need to buy a ticket to see the race from one of two main 'enclosures' (viewing areas). You might also want to set some money aside for the almost obligatory Pimm's and picnic of strawberries and cream.

For a paddle sport with a difference, consider boat racing Bangladeshi-style. **Nowka Bais** (nowkabaiscic.co.uk) is a traditional form of dragon boat racing and was rarely seen outside the Indian subcontinent until 2007, when Oxfordshire restaurateur Aziz Rahman introduced it to the Thames. He is convinced of its superiority to the Steve Redgrave sort of sport we're more used to seeing on our staider inland waterways. 'I don't want to say British rowing is boring, exactly,' he told me playfully when I interviewed

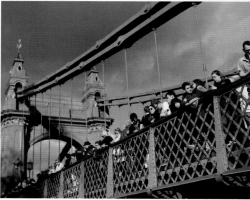

● (Above) *The University Boat Race takes place on the Thames in London and attracts good crowds along the length of the route.*

(Top Right) *Henley Royal Regatta is as much a social event as a sporting highlight.*

(Right) Bangladeshi boat racing offers noise, colour and cultural diversity.

him for *Waterways World* magazine in 2020, 'but Nowka Bais is just more of a spectacle. We aren't sitting down for a start – there's colour, headgear, music and singing. I thought something like that would be spectacular for the Thames.' Indeed, so successful was the first outing that the boats have been wheeled out annually for races ever since. The competition now attracts some 20,000 onlookers. While it's been held at Edgbaston Reservoir, Birmingham for the last few years, Aziz and his sons, who help organise the event, have their sights set on the Olympic rowing venue of Eton Dorney in future years, or even London Docklands.

Case study

GERARD WILCOX,
RECREATIONAL ROWER AND PRESIDENT
OF BURTON LEANDER ROWING CLUB

I joined Burton Leander Rowing Club in 1994 and go rowing once a week in an eight. Once we leave the landing stage we belong to a different world. The River Trent, alive and constantly moving, feels like a friend. The weekly outing gives me a good, strenuous workout and a chance to be active in unison with a group of friends. When the eight is moving quickly it is exhilarating. The boat sings. It is a little piece of frenetic, human activity in concert with the boat and the river that genuinely brings me a feeling of satisfaction and peace of mind.

As well as rowing, I also help with other tasks about the club, from mowing the lawn to being the club president. Three of my children have been members and the youngest, Michael (now 32), is still actively involved with rowing.

Our club has around 90 members, made up of 30 Juniors (ages 12 to 18), 50 active Seniors (ages 19 to 76!) and the rest social members. Of this number about 40 are female and 50 male. Long gone are the days of elitism and sexism in the sport – the place is a real 'community club' welcoming anyone who wants to row.

Saturday afternoons are for recreational rowing. There are about 20 of us who take part and afterwards we all linger at the club for tea and cake. The friendships made on and around the river are a core part of our club activity. It is a good place to be, with the river the common bond for us all.

Most members of this group are in their 40s, 50s and 60s. For some, joining the club was the first time they had rowed since university. For others, it was the first time they had rowed full stop. We will teach anyone how to row. ☛ burtonleanderrowingclub.co.uk

'The river feels like a friend'

Get your 'fix' elsewhere

Fixed-seat rowing (as opposed to the sliding-seat stuff mentioned earlier and seen at the Olympic and Paralympic Games) dates back to the very beginnings of water transport and it is fascinating to chart the way it has developed regionally around the UK, especially when it comes to the types of boats used. On the Thames, for example, skiffs, skerries and waterman cutters all class as traditional 'rowing boats' but vary in size, shape and construction, with some requiring rowers to use one oar, some two and some a mixture.

Fixed-seat rowing is a great sport, and growing fast in the UK. Skerries for Schools (skerries4schools.org), a charity established in 2014 to give secondary school students opportunities to try it, has bases in Richmond, Kingston and Reading. It says skerries are inherently more stable than sliding-seat craft, and easy to row and steer. The skerry also enables better interaction between coaches and rowers, allowing the former to move between rowers to help out when they run into difficulty or to demonstrate techniques. It is an unusual sport in that girls and boys can participate on the same team. Indeed, slightly more girls than boys take part.

For a recreational rowing boat experience, meanwhile, you generally don't have to look further than your nearest boating lake or honeypot riverside town to hire a craft for a couple of hours. Rowing isn't hard to get the hang of but if you're struggling to get anywhere fast don't be disheartened. One of the real joys of these boats is briefly shipping the oars, laying flat on your back in the bottom and letting it drift with the current, caring for nothing except the sky over your head.

● *Synonymous with summer fun, rowing boats can be hired at most honeypot sites on the waterways.*

BRITAIN'S BEST BOATING LAKES (AND RIVERS)

Serpentine, London

The Serpentine in Hyde Park is probably London's most famous boating lake and recently moved the operation of its craft in-house with a brand new fleet under The Royal Parks brand. Created in 1730 at the behest of Queen Caroline, the Serpentine was one of England's first artificial lakes that was designed to look natural rather than long and straight. It is named, in fact, for this snakelike feature.
☛ royalparks.org.uk

Henley-on-Thames, Oxfordshire

Home to the world-famous regatta, it would be a shame to visit this picturesque Thames town without having a go on the water yourself. Hobbs of Henley offers three- and five-seater fibreglass skiffs, which are pre-bookable for the whole day (from £80), or to 'turn up and hire'

by the hour (from £20). You can also order a picnic hamper to revive you for the journey back. A visit to the town's excellent River & Rowing Museum is also a 'must' while you're there.
☛ hobbsofhenley.com
rrm.co.uk

Stratford-upon-Avon, Warwickshire

(Right) All rowlocks, no Shylock, when you hire a boat from Shakespeare's birthplace. Avon Boating are conveniently placed near the RSC theatre, with small craft accommodating from four to six passengers and reasonably priced.
☛ avon-boating.co.uk

Durham, Northumberland

See Durham's historic cathedral and castle from a different angle with rowing boat hire on the River Wear. Prices are £8 per adult (plus a £10 deposit) and the boats are splendidly maintained.
☛ brownsboats.co.uk

Windermere and Coniston Water, Lake District

Indulge your inner Swallow or Amazon by rowing in the Lake District. Arthur Ransome claimed every location in his classic kids' adventure had a grounding in reality, with the lake loosely based on Windermere, and the surrounding countryside Coniston. Wild Cat Island itself draws on elements of both lakes:

(Above) *Rowing boats for hire on the River Avon in Stratford.*

(Below) *Explore the Brecon Beacons' Llangorse Lake by boat.*

Windermere's Blake Holme and Coniston's Peel Island.
☛ brockhole.co.uk
☛ conistonboatingcentre.co.uk

Loch Lomond, Scotland

A shorthand for rural Scottish beauty, Loch Lomond is the largest lake in Great Britain by surface area. You can explore it at your own pace from £25 per rowing boat, which will accommodate up to four people.
☛ lochlomond-scotland.com

Llangorse Lake, Brecon Beacons

(*Left*) Lovely Llangorse lies in a hollow formed by glacial action between the Central Beacons and the Black Mountains. It's belted by green hills, fields, meadows and hedgerows and has the only example in Wales of a crannog – an artificial island settlement more commonly found in Scotland and Ireland. As well as rowing boat hire, it's possible to rent a canoe, kayak, SUP, pedalo or fishing boat too.
☛ llangorselake.co.uk

Canoeing and kayaking

More so than most of the activities mentioned in this book, kayaking and canoeing demand that you're in tune with the movement of the water and the weather conditions you're paddling in. As such, it can be a much more immersive waterways experience and multiply some of the wellbeing benefits we've already covered. I once heard it described as at the intersection of meditation and adventure, and there's something about the focus required and the pure fun to be had that make this a good summing-up.

However it ultimately makes you feel, your first hurdle will be differentiating between the two sports, for 'kayaking' and 'canoeing' are not interchangeable – at least, not if you're talking to a semi-serious practitioner of either.

When it comes to recreational boating, think of canoes as the station wagons and kayaks the sports cars.

The former are more suited to families and couples as they can fit two or three people and carry larger loads for overnight camping trips. They're also often more practical – light enough to carry on your roof rack and made of hard-wearing plastic, so they can take a few knocks.

Kayaks are generally better suited to competitions and challenging water conditions. You tend to travel faster and they're usually built to carry fewer people. Also, while canoes commonly have an open deck for sitting or kneeling, a closed-cockpit kayak gives paddlers better protection from the elements and secure seating lower to the hull (bottom) of the boat, with your legs stretched forward.

Finally: your paddle. In a canoe this is typically a single-bladed one with a 'T-grip', but it wouldn't work quite so well propelling you on a kayak, where you're closer to the waterline. For that reason, kayak paddlers usually use a double-bladed one, which is suitable whether you are right- or left-handed.

How to get going

You can pick up a good-quality canoe for around £800–900 that will suit a novice paddler perfectly. Alternatively, look on eBay for cheaper second-hand boats. Bear in mind, however, that budget canoes tend to be heavy and more difficult to transport.

If you're worried about balance, remember that it's the width of the canoe that affects stability, so the larger the better for beginners. When comparing length, shorter canoes turn more easily but will likely be slower than a long, thin boat.

For kayaks, popular choices for newcomers include the sit on top (SOT) type, which are well suited to flat, sheltered waters, offer good stability, and are easy to get in and out of. Inflatable kayaks are also worth checking out if you're stuck for storage space and looking for something that's easy to transport. If you're feeling more adventurous, try a touring kayak.

These provide more comfort on longer journeys, plus space to carry your gear.

Once you've bought or borrowed a boat, remember to get it licensed. This paperwork relates to the boat itself, rather than being the waterways equivalent of a driving licence, so you won't have to jump through any hoops other than a straightforward online form to get it. It's required by most navigation authorities to access their rivers, canals and lakes, and costs £45 for the year when you purchase it through British Canoeing (britishcanoeing.org.uk) – but only if you live in England. If you're a resident of Wales see canoewales.com, or cani.org.uk for Northern Ireland. Scotland has the Right to Roam, which means you don't need a licence to paddle there, but joining the Scottish Canoe Association (canoescotland.org) is still advisable for a whole host of other benefits.

If you're new to canoeing or kayaking, I cannot recommend British Canoeing's brilliant Go Paddling website (gopaddling.info) enough. It includes overviews of all the main UK rivers, with routes, launches, trails, licensing information, plus pointers on wildlife and historic sites you might see while you're out. There's also the option to create and store your own trails, upload images, pinpoint hazards, and receive updates on your favourite waterways. If you'd rather follow tried and tested routes than DIY ones, you can search by location, trail type and difficulty level. Each suggestion contains times, local amenities and all the necessary safety information.

Go Paddling's blogs are equally worth a read, covering a huge breadth of topics. Need information on paddling on your period, while pregnant or through the menopause, for example? It's all there, and all good, considered advice.

Remember to get your kayak or canoe licensed before heading out on the water.

FOUR TO EXPLORE

Make a day of it – or more – with these great introductions to canoe touring. For any trip over two hours, remember to bring enough snacks and water (roughly 1.5 litres per person), a first-aid kit for minor injuries, a phone (in a waterproof pouch) for emergencies, a spare paddle, sunscreen and, for comfort, a back rest. If there's no watertight compartment in your boat, consider buying a 25-litre waterproof container to store this stuff instead.

1 River Wye

(Below) One of the country's most popular rivers for canoeing and kayaking (thanks in part to the number of commercial hire providers), the Wye is a fantastic place to get afloat for the first time and/or try a multi-day adventure. It winds its way from the Welsh mountains to join the River Severn at Chepstow and, for some of its length, gently delineates the border

between England and Wales. Particularly beautiful stretches include Builth Wells in Wales, but the whole length of the river is protected as a Site of Special Scientific Interest and, from Hereford onwards, you enter the Wye Valley Area of Outstanding Natural Beauty. Symonds Yat Rapids is one of the most iconic canoeing destinations in Britain, and now owned by British Canoeing. The organisation also owns a field in the village of Hoarwithy, roughly halfway between Ross-on-Wye and Hereford, which is well placed for an overnight wild camp.

2 Desmond Family Canoe Trail

(Below) The UK's first coast-to-coast canoe trail was opened in 2019 by the Canal & River Trust, who insist it is every bit as challenging and engaging as Alfred Wainwright's famous coast-to-coast walking counterpart. The 260km (162-mile) route, from Liverpool in the west

(Right) *The Desmond Family Canoe Trail includes locks and tunnels.*

(Left) *The River Wye is a draw for paddlers of all abilities.*

to Goole on the Humber estuary, takes in some of the key towns and villages that drove the Industrial Revolution, as well as incredible Pennine scenery. Paddlers can do as little or as much of the trail as they want but, with 91 locks to portage and a mile-long canal tunnel at Foulridge, it is not for the faint-hearted. Only more experienced paddlers should attempt the sections of the Aire & Calder Navigation.

3 River Tweed

Crossing the border between Scotland and England, this trail offers jaw-dropping countryside (especially through the Southern Uplands and moorland), plus areas of low-grade white water for those looking to stretch themselves a little. History buffs will be keen to explore Neidpath Castle, just west of Peebles, and, on the hillside above Dryburgh, the 6m- (20-foot)-high Wallace Monument to commemorate Braveheart himself.

4 River Blackwater Canoe Trail

This Northern Irish canoe trail is great for newbies, snaking 19km (12 miles) through the countryside of Armagh and Tyrone before finishing in Lough Neagh. And there are plenty of places to stop off for a bite to eat along the way to stretch out the idyllic day's paddle even longer. From Lough Neagh you can join another canoe trail along the beautiful River Bann all the way to the Atlantic, although some faster-flowing sections make this a little trickier to negotiate.

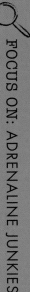

FOCUS ON: ADRENALINE JUNKIES

Do something every day that scares you, they say. Even if you don't subscribe to the 'every day' part of that dictum, it's hard to argue against the theory that looking fear in the face can build strength, resilience and confidence.

Nothing quite beats white-water rafting in that respect – effectively throwing a boat down an assault course and paddling furiously. You'll have a helmet, buoyancy aid, wetsuit and experienced guide, so it's a relatively safe way to get your thrills.

UK rivers are graded on a scale of I–VI, with VI offering the greatest navigational challenges. Most experiences hover somewhere in the middle, such as at the National White Water Centre in Bala, Wales (nationalwhitewatercentre.co.uk). Here, rafting takes place on the River Tryweryn on grade II–III rapids, with just one (easily portaged) grade IV on the lower stretch.

For a more literal adrenaline high, consider Pontcysyllte Aqueduct in Wales. The 38.4m- (126-foot)-high structure has no protective railing and is consequently out of bounds for stand-up paddleboarders on safety grounds, but canoeists are allowed to cross, as well as the nearby Chirk Aqueduct.

Case study

In 2015, celebrity gardener Alys Fowler embarked on a kayaking exploration of the Birmingham Canal Navigations to examine their flora and fauna. It spawned a critically acclaimed book, *Hidden Nature*, but more importantly gave her space to come to terms, aged 37, with the end of her marriage and the beginning of a new relationship.

Did you know much about the waterways of Birmingham before kayaking them?

Two of my friends had narrowboats, both moored in Gas Street Basin, so I'd sometimes go and hang out there with them, but not really. I knew the obvious stretches, like the bit around University and Gas Street Basin, but I hadn't explored them properly. To be honest, I had no idea back then that the network in Birmingham was as big as it is.

How soon into your kayaking journeys did you realise they would make great content for a book?

Initially I was just looking for a bit of adventure, without any idea to write about it. I wanted to say I'd explored some of Birmingham's canals, but quite quickly realised what a fantastic space they were. That was when I decided to write something, and started making notes about my trips as I paddled.

What was it about canal exploration that particularly appealed?

Once I'd moved past the really obvious bits and reached the parts that people don't go to as much, you suddenly realise that canals are as good as a park in terms of being immersed in nature in the middle of a city. I must confess I didn't have a great interest in the navigation side of things (although that's since changed after reading more books on narrowboating and the BCN's history). Instead, I was driven to explore the BCN because it felt like an unpeopled place.

The journeys correlated with quite a lot of personal upheaval, so the solitude must have been a big draw...

Yes, with hindsight it seems really obvious why I went there, but at the time it didn't feel the case. I didn't knowingly go there thinking that I needed to find solitude, but once I was there I appreciated it. As anyone who's spent time on a canal knows, there are quite long stretches where you can be completely alone with your thoughts.

*'There are quite long stretches
where you can be completely
alone with your thoughts'*

**How did you decide on an inflatable kayak
as the best craft to get afloat, and what
advantages does it have if you're looking to
get close to nature?**

*Well, mine's bright red so that negated some
advantages of an unpowered craft – quite a lot
of birds were very wary of it. They got more
accustomed to it on the bits I paddled regularly,
but it would have been much more sensible to have bought a green
boat instead. I was driven entirely by the fact I needed to be able to carry
the boat myself. There are cheaper blow-up kayaks, but you either need two
people to carry them or a car to get anywhere with them. I wanted something
that allowed me to be free to go as I please. It's not very fast, nor a necessarily
efficient boat for flat water. I often feel a bit like a waddling duck in it – you're
not very elegant – but there's the joy of being able to take it anywhere. The
paddle breaks down into four parts and the boat itself packs down into a
45-litre rucksack – a comfortable day pack.*

How kayak-friendly are Birmingham's waterways?

*Well, they're flat water so you'd have to be pretty incompetent to fail on them
– it's not like there are many obstacles. You're only allowed through a lock if
you have a motorised boat, so the challenge is climbing in and out a lot. That
was another appealing aspect of my boat – it's very light to portage. I think if
you were using a more traditional canoe or kayak that was made more solidly,
you'd definitely want to look at your route beforehand and take locks into
consideration.*

What makes the BCN so special?

*I suppose, because it's so old and narrow, the BCN has a real charm that you
don't find in a city like London, where the canals were built much wider to
maximise traffic. London's turn into a different space somehow as a result –
they become more like a very dull river. Birmingham's, though, have this lovely
feeling of being somewhere completely separate. Another thing that makes
the BCN different is that there are just so many waterways here and, because
they're not developed right the way up to the edge, they genuinely have this
feeling of being wild in a different way. Whether they'll be like that in 50 years'
time, or even 20 years' time, I don't know, but right now they're glorious.*

Adapted from an interview in *Waterways World*, May 2017, and reproduced with that magazine's kind permission.

9 SLEEP TIGHT

Swing in a hammock at the water's edge,
become an island castaway, or overnight
in luxury aboard a floating hotel

Trouble sleeping? Then perhaps you're among the growing number of people turning to noise aids to help drift off at night. You can listen to them on a smartphone app – they work by playing white noise or replicating things you'd hear in nature to soothe people to sleep and mask distracting sounds elsewhere (car horns, the neighbour's dog barking, etc).

Among the most consistently popular tracks are the watery ones – babbling brooks, rainfall and rushing waterfalls. These gentle, lulling sounds with gradual variations in the intensity of the moving water are the exact opposite of the loud, abrupt noises that tend to wake us up in a panic. The rhythmic splashing of water on to sand and rock can also be strangely meditative.

They are the sound of non-threats, at a basic level, but also do funny things to our notion of time – almost erasing it altogether. Hearing water murmur and coo as we lie in our beds feels the antithesis of the dreaded tick-tocking clock, which reminds us only that precious minutes of slumber are running away from us before a new day dawns, with the same old grey exhaustion.

Of course, it's not just how water sounds that makes it a light sleeper's salvation, but the rocking movement it creates too, as anyone who has slept on a boat will attest. In 2019, scientists from the Department of Neuroscience

Being cradled on the water can be conducive to a better sleep.

● Vätten Hüs in Manchester boasts whimsical floral arrangements on the ceiling and plenty of room.

at the University of Geneva studied this more closely on a group of 18 healthy young volunteers, who spent two nights sleeping in their lab. One of the nights was spent in a moving bed, and the other on the same bed, but in a still position. In both cases, the participants slept well. However, the researchers observed that they fell asleep more quickly – and had longer periods of deep sleep – when they were rocked.

Boat B&Bs

Anyone looking to benefit from this science should look no further than Beds on Board (bedsonboard.com), the website attempting to do for moored boats what Airbnb has done for houses and flats (although Airbnb now also offers plenty of houseboat options of its own). The site's modus operandi is simple: to connect boatowners and accommodation seekers. So no charters, no licensing, just beds on board.

Staying moored in one place makes this type of rental the perfect way to experience a bed afloat for the first time, and guests are encouraged to ask the boatowner any questions beforehand. But if you'd rather sleep in a boat B&B 'proper' than kip down in someone else's vacant cabin, plenty of static hotel-boats have cropped up around the system in recent years offering increasingly luxurious standards of accommodation. Among my favourites is London's **The Boathouse** (boathouselondon.co.uk), moored next to Paddington Basin's picturesque floating pocket park and (no surprise given it was launched in partnership with interior design brand Made) packing a chic punch with the decor. There's also a complimentary breakfast hamper on arrival, and bicycles and a rowing boat thrown in on which to explore the Big Smoke.

London's not the only city doing floating accommodation in style. In Manchester you can hop aboard the equally lavish **Vätten Hüs** boat (@thevattenhus), with its art deco inspired finishes, showstopping floral displays on the ceiling, king-sized bedrooms and open-plan kitchen/living space. There's also an outdoor deck for guests to soak up the sun with a drink.

Camping options

For a more traditional overnight stay on water, **Thames Skiff Hire** (skiffhire. com) is probably your best bet. A popular holiday activity in the 19th century (look no further than *Three Men in a Boat*), skiffs are essentially wooden rowing boats measuring about 9 metres (26 feet) long, built for ease of handling. At night, a canvas cover converts the entire craft into a snug tent with room for three people to sleep aboard. Equally useful, the cover can also provide weather protection during the day. Thames Skiff Hire have an enviable fleet – many of their classic craft have graced the silver screen, including the Harry Potter movies and *Shakespeare in Love*.

If you can't find a bed on the water, setting up next to it is a good second best. Technically, wild camping is prohibited in England, Wales and Northern Ireland (but not in Scotland), so if you're planning to pitch by the towpath or a riverbank you'll have to have the landowner's permission. Some sites in Scotland, including Loch Lomond, now require campers to get a permit during spring/summer, so do your research before you go. Checking the weather forecast is also strongly advised before setting off to ensure your kit is up to the challenge.

The cardinal rule of wild camping is to be as discreet as possible. This generally means arriving late and leaving early, only staying one night, keeping groups very small (only one or two tents) and taking all litter home with you. Even if there's evidence that fires have been lit at the site previously, don't be tempted to start your own. If you need a heat source for cooking, use a stove instead of a campfire or disposable BBQ.

Water is heavy to carry, so the temptation to use the river or lake you're camped by as a drinking supply will be great. Remember that running water is generally safer than still and is best collected as close to the source as possible.

Be sure to check immediately upstream for animal carcasses or waste, and boil any water before drinking or use a tried-and-tested water filter.

While it pains me to bring up the subject of toilet requirements, it's important when camping by rivers, lakes or streams that you perform these duties a good distance away from the water and bury the results with a trowel.

Finally, it's worth remembering that water attracts midges, so make sure you invest in good bug protection.

For a slightly tamer night's sleep, consider a conventional campsite: there's a good list of waterside ones on Cool Camping's website (coolcamping.com/campsites/waterside-camping), but the bible really is Stephen Neale's *Camping by the Waterside: The Best Campsites by Water in Britain and Ireland*. Now in its second edition, it covers all kinds of camping (caravan, campsite and wild), with tips on how to plan your trip and what gear to take, as well as being stuffed full of tempting site

recommendations. You might also consider joining the Camping and Caravanning Club, the oldest camping organisation in the world, or the Caravan and Motorhome Club. They cost from £45 to £56 per year, for which you'll be able to access their entire campsites network, including thousands of smaller privately owned sites that are exclusive to members, plus save a tidy sum per night by no longer paying the non-member fee.

Look, too, at the National Trust's portfolio of sites. It's not a 'camping' association, of course, but it does own a large number of places to pitch a tent or park a caravan, many of which are close to stunning lakes and rivers. One of its newest acquisitions is Cloud Farm at Lynton, Exmoor, an area made famous by the 19th-century novel *Lorna Doone* by RD Blackmore. You can choose a pitch right next to Badgworthy Water, a river that (in Blackmore's words) glides 'with a soft dark babble', and hike out to other spots featured in the book.

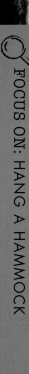

Favoured by sailors since the Elizabethan navy formally adopted them in 1597, hammocks have quite a history among boaty types. Indeed, many sailors became so accustomed to their 'hanging cabins' that they brought them ashore with them on leave. As well as the obvious attraction of being gently swayed to sleep, hammocks also keep you off damp ground and away from (most) critters.

You'll be spoilt for choice when it comes to buying one, from simple single-skin nylon affairs to contraptions that are more akin to suspended tents, with zipped access and integral bug nets.

If you've never tried a hammock before, buy the biggest you can afford. Being squeezed top and bottom where the ends are pulled in is no fun, and remember that a more comfortable night will be had if there's room to sleep diagonally. You might also invest in a foam or inflatable mat to lie on, to avoid loss of body heat and being chilled by moving air beneath you.

When it comes to hanging your hammock, long, flat tree straps are the least damaging to trunks and mean you don't have to master any tricky knots. Look for straps that have a loop on one end and multiple attachment points sewn along the length. Simply place the single-loop end around the tree, then insert the long end of the strap through and pull tight. Next, clip a carabiner to any one of the attachment points, repeat the whole process on the other tree, and you should be ready to go.

Check the manufacturer's directions for ideal hanging distances, but the general rule of thumb is about 0.6 metres (2 feet) longer than the total length of a hammock (measured from the hanging points). Don't suspend it more than 40 to 50cm (16 to 19 inches) above the ground if you can help it, and definitely avoid hanging it over water.

If you want a gentle introduction to hammock camping next to water, **Y'Gelli** (ygellicamping.co.uk), based in Llanybydder, Carmarthenshire, boasts 8 acres of woodland with glorious views across the River Teifi. Its hammock pitches cost £15 per person per night, including use of a fire pit, drinking water and Portaloo. You can also hire a hammock at the site itself if you don't have your own.

SLEEP TIGHT

ISLAND HOPPING

Britain's rugged coastline boasts plenty of island escapes for wannabe castaways, but few people consider that our lakes and rivers can offer just as magical an overnight experience, albeit on a necessarily smaller scale.

Loch Maree

(Below) Loch Maree, in Wester Ross in the north-west Highlands, is the fourth-largest freshwater loch in Scotland, and the largest north of Loch Ness. It contains five sizeable wooded islands and over 60 smaller ones. Once you've got your head around the sheer number of them, consider that the biggest island, Eilean Sùbhainn, contains a loch that itself contains an island – something that's unique in the whole of Great Britain.

The islands are home to countless species of plant, insect and bird, including otters and black-throated divers. As such, they're protected by National Nature Reserve designation and there are restrictions on when you can camp here. It is forbidden from April to August, to avoid disturbance to unseen nests, so plan around that or book a local campsite instead during those months. No fires, BBQs or fire pits are allowed on any of the islands at any time of year.

Lough Erne

(Right) In Northern Ireland, Lough Erne is also a haven for wild camping and there are several potential sites identified in the trail guide on CanoeNI's website (www.canoeni.com/canoe-trails/lough-erne/camping-facilities/). They are free to use but, as is the nature of 'rough' camping, have no facilities. There are also, however, a number of official campsites offering toilets and showers etc. These should be booked in advance.

Moat Island Glamping, Norfolk

(Below, right) To Norfolk next, for something rather more genteel – a campsite surrounded by what was once a medieval moat. Just 16km (10 miles)

north of Norwich, Moat Island Glamping is on the site of old Haveringland Hall and comprises five Lotus Belle tents, each sleeping up to five people and kitted out with double beds, wood burners and, in the two 'stargazer' tents, clear ceiling panels to take in the night sky before getting your shut-eye. But Moat Island's pièce de résistance is the naturally filtered swimming pond and jetty. The water is 2 metres (6½ feet) deep with native plants along the shallow sides, which attract dragonflies that rollick along as you swim.

☛ moatisland.co.uk

Monkey Island, Thames

For all-out luxury, visit Monkey Island, the 18th-century estate turned boutique retreat on a private island on the Thames in the village of Bray, Berkshire. The Thames lays claim to almost 200 eyots and islands, many with a fascinating history. This one is no exception. Originally a medieval monastery, it was bought by the 3rd Duke of Marlborough as a fishing retreat in 1723 and became a popular place for visitors to dine and stay from the 19th century. Now expensively revamped, guests can enjoy beautifully landscaped gardens and picturesque views of the river, as well as a novel floating spa concept on a converted canal boat. Among treatments available is a 60-minute 'floating massage' on a specially designed aqua-cushion treatment bed.

☛ monkeyislandestate.co.uk

● (Above) *Magical Lough Erne has more than 150 islands.*

(Left) *Camping on Loch Maree's islands is only allowed at certain times of the year.*

(Below) *Make a splash at Moat Island Glamping in Norfolk.*

Case study

JASPER WINN, ADVENTURER AND AUTHOR OF
WATER WAYS: A THOUSAND MILES ALONG BRITAIN'S CANALS

There's the Huckleberry Finn romance of making the waterside your bed, and there's also the pleasingly practical side of kipping out canal-side or on a riverbank.

My revelatory journey of waterways discovery was a thousand-mile kayak trip on rivers and canals across Ireland, England and France, from Dublin to the Mediterranean. Nineteen years old, paddling a cheap kayak, tentless and with barely enough money to eat, each night's camp was a blanket on the ground, bread and cheese, and a small campfire. The freedom and simplicity was intoxicating. And the key to future travels.

Decades, and numerous river and waterways and coastal journeys later, I set off to spend a year cycling, walking and paddling Britain's canals to research the book *Water Ways*. Most nights I made the waterside my bedroom, still bivvying sleeping rather than using a tent.

I want to describe the magic of waking at very early dawn and hearing the birds that make the waterways their home start to move and chatter. The relief of making a snug camp on a filthy night and watching the weather unfold while lying warm and dry. The sheer animal pleasure of dropping to the ground after a long day's walk, knowing I was 'home' for the night.

Well, I want to describe them all, but the truth is that those who know how it feels to sleep out by the water need no telling and already have their personal experience to draw on. While for those who haven't tried it yet, then the only useful words are of encouragement.

And some advice. Use common sense. Have respect for the natural world and other people. Ask permission to sleep out where practical, and where one can't then make camp late, leave early and leave no trace. Sometimes, in hot summer weather, I've walked at night and slept during the day, needing less kit, having the towpath to myself, seeing more wildlife and looking like an innocent idler when asleep in the midday sun.

Above all, head to the waterside and go to bed.

☛ @theslowadventure

*'The freedom and simplicity
was intoxicating'*

10 HITCH A RIDE

From modern work commutes to centuries-old ferry crossings, functional river transport can be full of fun too

'Commuting: The stress that doesn't pay' ran the headline of a *Psychology Today* article in 2015 all about the absolute dirge that is getting to work. The bleak feature was a catalogue of the many and varied ways the practice conspires to swindle us of time, money and happiness. Boredom, anger, a sense of loss of control, stress, social isolation, impatience, fatigue and frustration were all listed as unwanted side effects, and the author also pointed out how it can sabotage time better spent sleeping in, exercising, with family, or simply prepping a healthy lunch.

But then, wham, just as the full extent of our Faustian bargain has sunk in, a chink of light… Play your commuting cards right, the article acknowledges, and there can actually be an upside to the get-to-work hustle. It could even – audible gasp – make you… happy?

While much of the focus thereafter is given to 'active commuting' (ie walking or cycling), public transport can still be a runner when it comes to boosting mental wellbeing. Compared to journeying by car (what's termed a 'non-passive travel mode', requiring constant concentration), passengers on public transport have time to relax. This is key, researchers say, to transforming time in transit to something we actually desire, not just endure.

Commuter boats

If packed buses and trains make the theory a little hard to swallow, there is a massively less contentious alternative in cities that benefit from proximity to water. London and its **Thames Clippers** service (thamesclippers.com) is the obvious example.

The company was founded in 1999 and began with one boat servicing 80 passengers a day between Greenland (Rotherhithe) and Savoy piers. Since then, the fleet has grown substantially and now has 20 vessels serving 24 piers across four routes.

Just like the Tube and buses, passengers are able to use their Oyster card for the ride, and can even add some self-determination to the commute by pre-booking on the firm's app.

For Samantha Campbell, the company's head of marketing, the boats don't just offer 'an exciting, unique and convenient commuting experience', but also something that's 'stress-free' and, even more astonishingly in the context of getting to the office, 'luxurious' too. Comfortable, guaranteed seats, climate-controlled cabins with incredible views, barista-made coffee and even a reliable phone signal. No wonder the marketing team's #loveyourcommute hashtag is working well on social media.

Uber Boat by Thames Clippers carried 2.44 million passengers in 2021, representing a 57 per cent like-for-like increase compared with 2019 pre-Covid passenger numbers and exceeding the performance of many other public transport modes in London during the pandemic.

Thames Clippers provide a convenient and uncrowded way into work for Londoners.

Case study

I've been using Thames Clippers on and off since 2009. I lived in Sydney for a while before that, and I used the ferries there to get to work, which I suppose put the idea in my head. When I moved back to London, it wasn't yet an option to commute by boat, so I had to get the train and Tube, and I hate the Tube. I find it claustrophobic, and either too hot or too cold. It's just awful.

I get the boat from Putney Pier to London Bridge City Pier, and that takes an hour. I walk down to the boat, which is obviously good exercise, and walk to my office when I get off at the other side too.

In the mornings they sell tea and coffee aboard. One of the baristas is particularly good. Even if you didn't see him for a year, he'd still remember exactly how you like your tea, find you on the boat, and let you pay later in the journey. In the evenings they have a full bar. It sells everything – beer, wine, spirits, sandwiches. It's amazing.

Initially I envisaged I'd spend the commute with my nose in a book, but there's just so much to see. Every day is different – that's what I love about the water. And the sights are never-ending. You can watch birds (and helicopters!) landing and taking off, see cargo vessels going up and down, get close enough to the Houses of Parliament to make out MPs having a drink on the balcony. There are certain sights that you can only see from the river, and I still have to pinch myself that I'm privy to them, and all for the price of an ordinary commuter fare. Every day I see something new that makes me smile or laugh.

It's so interesting watching my colleagues come into work off the Tube. They're often late, they look stressed, they invariably moan about how busy it was, and in summer they're dripping in sweat. And they say: 'Why

'It's the only time you'll hear anyone say the commute is the best part of their day'

are you smiling?' Well, because I've spent the last hour sitting outside watching an amazing sunrise. The number of people who tell me they wish they could get the ferry too. So I get out the map and show them that in plenty of cases it's possible.

Usually people dread their commute, but this trip is something I do even if I'm not going into work. It's the highlight of my day. I suppose it's just more civilised. Everyone is polite and smiles at you (probably because we're all guaranteed a seat) and it's more congenial. The staff are wonderful too. They always greet you with a 'good morning' and thank you for using the service as you disembark, or wish you a good day. Those small things really make a difference. It's the only time you'll hear anyone say the commute is the best part of their day.

I like my job, don't get me wrong, and I work with nice people, but I look forward to getting on the boat at the end of the day. Often my colleagues will shout out the door: 'Enjoy the ferry, have a beer on me while I'm on the Tube.' You can hear the envy in their voice. I love that.

 Commute with a view: the Houses of Parliament from a Thames Clipper.

Ferry across the Mersey – and beyond

Other cities have their own water-based options. Workers in Liverpool, Birkenhead and the Wirral have long had the **Mersey Ferries** (*Below bottom*), while Bristolians can call upon iconic blue-and-yellow **Bristol Ferry Boats** (*Below top*) or a cross-harbour craft called *Mary Brunel*, which is operated by **Number Seven Boat Trips** and was co-designed by James Dyson of bagless-vacuum-cleaner fame while he was still a student at the Royal College of Art.

In **Leeds**, two boats named *Twee* and *Drie* ferry 120,000 passengers across the River Aire between Leeds Dock and the train station every year for just £1 per person. A TaxiTrak app lets you track the boats' movements in real time, so you can even avoid time-wasting waits for the service.

And north of the border, **Glasgow City Council** is reportedly looking at the feasibility of launching commuter boat travel on the Forth & Clyde Canal with a water bus. A council paper said it would help link communities on each side of the 11 miles of the waterway within Glasgow.

Inland ferries obviously exist outside of urban areas too. And with many operators demanding little more than loose change for the privilege, using these services can be a fun way to get afloat for the whole family, albeit briefly. A particularly charming example

(Above) *The blue-and-yellow blur of a Bristol Ferry boat.*

(Below) *Ferry across the Mersey.*

is the chain ferry at **Normanton-on-Soar** in Nottinghamshire. Relaunched in April 2017, the service is hand-operated seasonally by volunteers and costs just £1 each way (dogs and bikes 50p). The ferry has a long history: in existence since 1771, it provided a crossing from the Nottinghamshire village to the fields of Leicestershire and, as such, a faster route to Zouch and Loughborough. It was a well-chosen site – silt and debris deposits on the slow-moving bend made this one of the shallowest points on the stretch of river, and there's speculation it may have even been possible to ford during hot, dry summers.

Packed steamers throng the Thames in Victorian London.

Water wellness the Victorian way

Of course, you don't need the excuse of the 9–5 to catch a ride on a passenger boat – they can (and should) be enjoyed for their own sake too. The Victorians knew this better than most – indeed, we owe the 19th century a great debt for shining a light on these craft as leisure amenities as well as workhorses.

The Victorians were just good with water full stop, weren't they? Think of a British seaside holiday, for example, and nearly all the best bits (taking a dip, messing about in the sand etc) are just lazy copies of what these forebears made fashionable. And so it is on our inland waterways too, reaching a zenith between 1830 and 1860 when the Thames was swarming with boat trips, regattas, picnics and general jollity.

Steamboat services (*Above*), in particular, seized the public imagination like nothing before. They opened up new parts of the river for the working classes of the capital who, come weekends and holidays, took the seats previously occupied by commuters and fled the Big Smoke for the green banks and fresh air of the Home Counties instead. Estimates put the number of steamers working on the river by 1844 at 200.

Today, we can still tap into these leisure and wellbeing trips the Victorians were so mad about. Based at Folly Bridge, Oxford, directly overlooking the river, **Salters** (salterssteamers.co.uk) was founded in 1858 and initially made its name producing racing sculls, supplying top-class rowing eights to Oxford and Cambridge universities for the annual Boat Race. But come 1888, the company had expanded into scheduled passenger

139

trips up and down the non-tidal Thames, starting with a service that ran between Oxford and Kingston, stopping overnight at hotels along the route. The trip took two days going downriver and three days to return. The towns of Abingdon, Wallingford, Reading, Henley, Marlow, Windsor and Staines provided excellent stopping-off points on the way and passengers were able to choose how far they wished to travel along the route. The concept was a hit and the passenger fleet began to expand.

Dozens of steamers were built by Salters until production ended in 1931. Over the years the size of the vessels grew, with *Mapledurham* and *Cliveden* barely fitting into some of the smaller locks of the upper Thames.

Salters still runs some of this original fleet alongside more modern craft. The steam engines were removed in the 1950s and 60s but the boats retain plenty of other heritage features to make 21st-century passengers feel like they're dipping a toe in the past.

The run from Oxford to Abingdon is a great taster, with highlights including the Oxford University intercollegiate regatta course and the magnificent Nuneham House. The journey also links two hugely popular waterside pubs – the Head of the River at Oxford and Nag's Head at Abingdon.

Yarmouth Belle *is operated by Turks Thames Cruises, a 300-plus-year-old, family-run, Thames riverboat company.*

Providing a similar service further downstream is the **River Thames Boat Project** (thamesboatproject.org), a charity catering for people of all ages, including those with a special need, disability or mental health condition. It offers 'therapeutic cruises' as either day trips or longer residential affairs covering the Windsor to Putney stretch, as well as educational days.

RTBP was formed in 1988 when the then mayor of Richmond, Martin Emerson, and an energetic team of supporters acquired a 30-metre (100-foot) Dutch barge, built in 1908, which they subsequently renamed *Thames Venturer*. The charity was registered in 1989 and, soon after, the focus of a *Challenge Anneka* TV show enabled the boat to be fitted out with a galley, saloon and lift, transforming her into the accessible community boat she is today.

A second craft was added in 2018 to expand the number of river excursions on offer. This custom-built day-boat features a sunny front deck and large panoramic windows, helping passengers feel even closer and more connected to the water.

Case study

JULIAN KENNARD, RELIEF
PASSENGER BOAT SKIPPER

'I'm the best version of myself on the river'

I was 11 years old when I fell in love with the Thames. I was sitting with my parents aboard our hire cruiser when the languid sound of jazz drifted through the amber haze of an early autumn evening and my ears pricked up. As I turned my head to the direction of the music, a beautifully shaped boat came into view and, according to my mother, my eyes opened as wide as saucers. The elegant Edwardian passenger steamer, thronged with jolly musicians and swaying revellers, was unquestionably the most beautiful thing I had ever seen. As it slipped past our mooring, I resolved to find a way to get aboard myself one day.

And so it was, eight years later during a gap year before university, that I gained my qualifications as a Class V passenger vessel skipper and took command of the same fleet of 'Salter's Steamers', as they are affectionately known. There is really nothing that compares to experiencing this magical river aboard something that is itself a piece of history. Many passengers come back again and again, a number have their favourite steamer and even their favourite seat from which to observe a part of life you simply won't see anywhere else. For me, the best part of the job is seeing someone local step aboard for the very first time. Afterwards, they invariably tell me they can't believe what they've missed in their backyard all this time.

I still regularly take the helm, when my day job and family commitments allow me that time to be in 'my happy place'. It feels like my natural environment and provides space for me to be the best version of myself. I am as much in love with it as I ever was.

BUCKET LIST BOAT TRIPS

We don't need scientists to tell us that experiential diversity (that is, going to new or different places and doing different things) can make us feel happier. Exposure to novelty has long been associated with wellbeing and positive emotions – it's the reason we look forward to holidays so much, or plan elaborate treats to mark special occasions. When it comes to pushing the (passenger) boat out and trying something new, you can't go far wrong with any of these suggestions:

The great Great Glen explorer cruise

(*Left*) For sheer majesty of the views, you probably won't beat **Lord of the Glens**' (lordoftheglens.co.uk) Caledonian and Great Glen Explorer cruise. On the five-night trip from Inverness to Oban, you'll be treated to hauntingly beautiful Highland scenery and top-notch cuisine aboard one of Scotland's most elegant cruise ships and the only passenger boat able to navigate both the country's inland waterways and the open sea.

The downside is that all this splendour comes at a price – from £1,700 per person, to be precise. If that's stretching your budget, look at Scottish Canals' (scottishcanals.co.uk) list of boating holidays and day trips on the Caledonian Canal instead. Among the cheaper options are a two-hour trip sampling Thomas Telford's famous canal and the legendary water of Loch Ness with **Jacobite Cruises** for just £26 per person. The brilliant **Seagull Trust**'s (seagulltrust.org.uk) Highland branch, meanwhile, offers free Caledonian Canal cruising for those with special needs.

Horse around on the Grand Western Canal

Horse-boating takes the modish concept of 'slow travel' to the extreme. But Tiverton Canal Co (www.tivertoncanal.co.uk/), which operates along the beautiful Grand Western Canal in Devon, insists it's the ultimate way to relax and unwind from the stress of modern living, and I quite agree. In the 'heyday' of canals, thousands of horses were hitched up to boats to haul goods along our inland

waterways, but today the Tivertonian is one of only a small handful of craft that are still pulled this way and open to the public. The company offers 1.5 and 2.5-hour return trips from the wharf in Tiverton (starting at £15.90 for adults) from April until October.

The canal itself is pretty special too. Now owned by Devon County Council and managed as both a country park and a local nature reserve, it previously stretched as far as Taunton in Somerset, and was largely used for the carriage of limestone. These days it is only navigable for 18km (11 miles) but some 300,000 visitors still come here to enjoy the wildlife, fishing and other leisure amenities.

Have a blast to the Thames Barrier

(*Right*) A chilly February morning probably wasn't the best time for me to test out **Thames RIB Experience**'s (thamesribexperience.com) high-speed, 75-minute boat service through central London to the Thames Barrier. I was grateful, as were the nine other intrepid-but-teeth-chattering passengers lined up on Embankment Pier, that our introduction to high-octane river thrills came via a thorough wardrobe makeover. Waterproof trousers were optional – the insulated all-weather jackets, complete with nose and mouth covers and hoods, were not. A lifejacket completed the transformation from casual London tourist to something more suited to polar exploration, all in under 10 minutes.

The boats are incredibly high-spec – all 740hp of a twin-turbo-engined rigid inflatable, a craft more usually favoured for Special Forces action than city centre pleasure cruising. You'll reach a top speed of 30 knots from Wapping Police Station (12-knot restrictions apply through central London) – the thrills enhanced by tight, snaking turns. Along the way, iconic London sights are pointed out via quirky, often tongue-in-cheek commentary that segues well into the James Bond theme tunes blasting from the speakers. The Thames Barrier experience will set you back £57 per adult, but there are shorter, cheaper trips available too.

If you feel the need for speed elsewhere on our inland waterways system, try the Loch Lomond Speedboat Pub Tour from Luss Pier (*Left*) (lochlomond-scotland.com/boat-tours/speedboat-pub-tour). There are different options depending on how many pubs you wish to visit and whether or not you'll be dining, but the standard is three hours, three pubs, which costs £360 for a small boat (six adults) or £450 for a big boat (ten adults). Passengers can avail themselves of waterproof, fleece-lined ponchos to keep out the chill zipping over the water to the next pint.

(Above) *Hold on tight for the Thames RIB Experience.*

(Top left) *The Caledonian Canal cuts through the spectacular Great Glen.*

(Left) *See the highlights of Loch Lomond on a speedboat pub crawl.*

A horse-drawn boat trip on the Grand Western Canal in Devon.

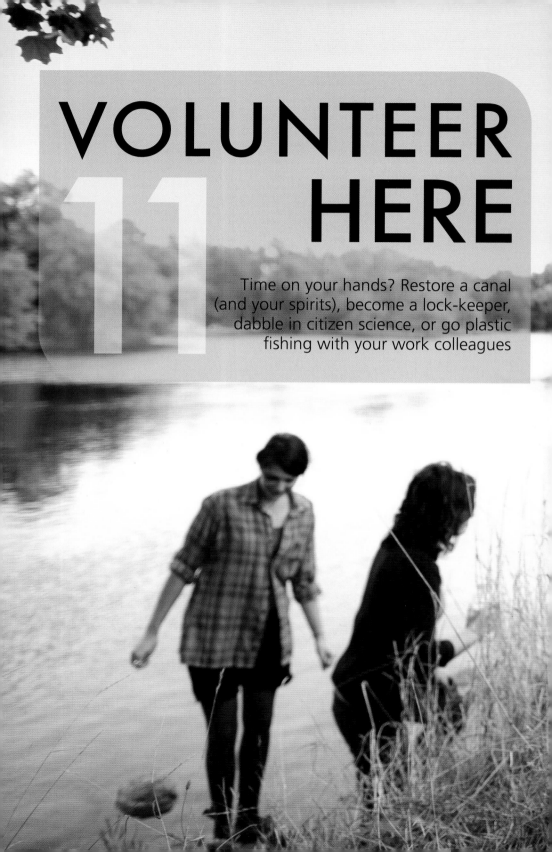

VOLUNTEER HERE

11

Time on your hands? Restore a canal (and your spirits), become a lock-keeper, dabble in citizen science, or go plastic fishing with your work colleagues

W hen the pandemic hit and the world locked down, many of us looked back on those last weeks of normality with the intensity of nostalgia usually reserved for teenage love affairs and lost childhoods. But even without the Covid context, I think I would have pined for one particular March 2020 morning, because it had started with so little promise – a workboat on the Coventry Canal, in discouraging cold and unflattering PPE, chainsawing overhanging vegetation with complete strangers – and ended with a genuine reluctance to leave and repeated promises to return soon.

The Inland Waterways Association's Lichfield branch has been fielding an offside vegetation team, supported by Canal & River Trust staff, on its local waterways since January 2018. For CRT, the navigation authority charged with maintaining these canals, the benefits are blindingly obvious – a trained volunteer workforce helps it stay on top of an already gargantuan winter works programme and keep associated costs (as much as £1.7m a year) down.

But until that morning, when I was tasked with joining in for a *Waterways World* feature, I found it difficult to understand the motivation for the people who turned up – the five to eight volunteers who devote two days a week to it, from late autumn to spring, fielding numb fingers, horrid weather, bramble splinters and a mob of power tools. Sure, there was the jokey suggestion that 70-something-year-old Heather's chocolate cake for elevenses was more than worth forsaking duvets and braving the dark mornings, but having grown up around Lichfield and its glut of cafés, I wasn't wholly convinced that wielding pole saws was the only way to procure a good mid-morning snack.

There's much more to it. Countless studies in recent years have underlined the huge wellbeing benefits that come with giving up our time to help others, even if cutting unruly saplings on a deserted towpath is the sort of do-gooding that rarely gets a direct thank you. For a start, volunteering can help people feel more socially connected to others. This camaraderie is something all the volunteers I spoke to that morning cited as the biggest lure, but there were plenty more perks I hadn't considered. For Neil, the group's organiser, there was the fresh air, the free day's boating, the sense of achievement and getting out from under his wife's feet for a few hours.

All retirees, these volunteers also admitted the physical exercise was good for them. Watching Heather bail half-metre logs out of the water as easily as spooning sponge mix into her cake tins spoke for itself.

So I was better primed a year later, when CRT published a report revealing the economic and social value of volunteering to the organisation, to those who volunteer and to wider society. Trust volunteers, it said, display higher personal wellbeing statistics than the general sample of a similar age in the national comparison group. While volunteering can be good for anyone, it is particularly worthwhile, the report continued, for people in later years of life, those living with chronic physical health conditions and people with lower levels of wellbeing. In terms of mental health, it found the difference in anxiety to be particularly strong: CRT volunteers show lower anxiety than both non-volunteers and volunteers of a similar age and working status.

This evidence is borne out in numerous case studies on the charity's website. An extreme example is Sheila McGough, who was left with post-traumatic stress disorder after a violent

mugging, and too terrified to leave the house on her own. Therapy helped, but it was volunteering on her local towpath – making repairs, litter picking and putting in stock fencing – that she credits with bringing her confidence back and giving her 'a second family' and sense of purpose.

It's often dirty work but volunteering on your local canal or river can do wonders for your mental wellbeing.

149

Getting started

Before committing to a project, think carefully about the waterways causes you care about and the skills and experience you can offer. Aligning a role with your passions and/or expertise will increase the chances of you enjoying it.

Next, you'll need to be realistic about how much time you can afford to devote to the position. It's best to begin with a fairly limited commitment (perhaps no longer than a couple of months) to make sure it suits you, and then upping your hours when you're sure you've the spare hours and continued enthusiasm.

Once you've settled on a position (and before applying), make sure you know all the details. Will training or special equipment be required? Will you have to travel far? If possible, talk to other people in the same role to gauge whether the day-to-day is any different from the task you imagine in your head.

After applying, don't feel defeated if you have to wait longer than anticipated for a response. Many non-profit organisations have limited staff resources so it can take a while for your expression of interest to be met with an invitation to chat further or get started. At the same time, don't be shy about sending a follow-up message to show you're still keen.

Once you're up and running, try to treat the role as you would a 'proper' paying job. That means being punctual, professional and delivering all you've promised. Hopefully it will be the start of a long and happy placement, making a positive difference to blue spaces that mean a lot to you and your local community. If, however, you find you're not enjoying it, or have any other concerns, talk to your volunteer coordinator about ways to improve the situation, or find out if there are roles within the organisation you might be better suited to.

'Bread and butter'

In terms of opportunities, clean-ups are the bread and butter of waterways volunteering, ensuring our rivers, lakes and canals are an attractive place for everyone to enjoy and in the best possible condition to support the wildlife that depends on them. The **Canal & River Trust's Towpath Taskforce** teams, for example, meet regularly on different stretches of the canal network in England and Wales to plant hedgerows, paint locks, tackle problem plants and litter pick. The **Inland Waterways Association** organises similar canal clean-ups and

work parties among its local branches. Meanwhile, the **Rivers Trust**, an umbrella organisation for 60 member trusts concerned with rivers in England, Wales, Northern Ireland and Ireland, says one of its most popular volunteer events is 'balsam bashing', to rid the waterways of Himalayan balsam and other invasive species. 'It's an incredibly therapeutic activity', the group says, 'and great for letting off some steam.'

If you're part of a watersports club, you'll find other ways to be involved, from coaching and repairing equipment to just making the tea.

Other opportunities can be more site-specific. Scotland's largest urban nature park, **Seven Lochs Wetland Park**, offers a variety of volunteer programmes. Comprising, as the name suggests, seven lochs, five local nature reserves, a country park and one of Glasgow's oldest buildings at Provan Hall, it also has miles of walking and cycling routes to explore. Volunteering is a good way to learn more about the park's heritage and nature, it says, while also helping to protect and improve the park. If you want to get your hands dirty, join the group that meets every Friday to carry out conservation projects. Alternatively, become a citizen scientist with the 'Wildlife Counts' initiative. You'll be helping to survey and monitor

the nature in the park – from counting birds, bees and butterflies to measuring frog spawn. The site is also looking for volunteer rangers to welcome visitors, show them what to look out for, and assist with events such as guided walks and family activities. Projects are supervised by experienced leaders, and no previous experience is needed.

If being outdoors isn't your thing, some navigation authorities and waterways charities advertise office-based roles (everything from marketing to governance roles), which often appeal to graduates looking for work experience or professionals considering a career change. There are also specialist volunteer roles to consider, which could include working on the education side of things, especially among children, or on environment and heritage teams.

If you're outgoing and sociable, a public-facing role might be best for you, not just welcoming people to the towpath or riverbank but also on volunteer teams at waterways museums and attractions.

● (Left) *Clean-up groups are widespread around the inland waterways network, and offer a common route into volunteering.*

(Below) *Sign up to monitor water quality or wildlife as a citizen scientist.*

Case study

GOING SOLO - ROSIE LANDERS

'Litter picking has improved my life greatly'

You don't have to be affiliated to a charity or navigation authority to make a difference on the waterways, as litter-picking Rosie Landers found out.

When I moved to Huddersfield, I saw straight away that it had lovely countryside and canals. However, every time I went for a walk I saw so much litter, on the paths and in the water. This had a negative effect on what was supposed to be a relaxing pastime, so I wondered if I could actually do something about it.

I bought an inexpensive grabber from a local DIY shop and started picking litter just on the driveway of my apartment complex (located on the edge of a canal). I then regularly started litter picking on my walks along the canal and in local woodland. I now litter pick about once a week; however, I go much less during the winter as it's not very fun in wet and windy weather.

Anyone can litter pick; you don't need fancy equipment, although if you would like to do it regularly and thoroughly I recommend buying a grabber and a hoop for holding the bin bag open, which I have found to be very handy.

Litter picking has improved my life greatly as I feel like I am making a positive difference to my local area, no matter how small. I also feel rewarded when I see the wildlife on the canal, knowing that at least I've done something to reduce the level of water pollution. Of course, it's also great exercise and generally good fun!

(Top and above left) *An Inland Waterways Association offside vegetation team, supported by Canal & River Trust staff.*

(Above right) *Keep your local blue spaces beautiful by volunteering to pick up plastic.*

Think outside the box

In some instances it's possible to combine waterways volunteering with another, entirely separate, interest in your life. A keen gardener? Then consider lending your talents to CRT's ambitious attempt to create the **longest orchard in the world** (*Below*), stretching 80km (50 miles) along the West Midlands' canal network and made up of 3,000 trees. In what is expected to be a ten-year project, the orchard will be planted with cherry, plum, apple and pear, including rare historic varieties, and exotic species such as peach, apricots, figs, persimmon, loquats and pomegranates. Once planted, the Trust will need people to help care for the towpath trees, to ensure they establish through the early years, produce fruit, and are used as a resource by the community.

Or perhaps you like walking, in which case volunteering as a monitor on the **Thames Path** might be just up your street, checking the condition of the trail's surface and any issues with gates and signs. Prefer running? I give you the Scandi-inspired **'plogging'** trend. A combination of jogging and litter picking, the portmanteau term was apparently first coined on Instagram in 2016. Participants say it gives them a focus and helps distract from the distance they're running. As it can be a bit awkward to run with a litter picker, it's best just to take a bag and gloves.

If you're struggling to find time to fit volunteering around a full-time job, try to persuade your boss to sign up for some corporate volunteering on the waterways. There are plenty of benefits for your organisation, from increasing workplace pride and staff retention to encouraging employees to work together and build relationships. Corporate volunteering can also give employees new skills, boosting self-esteem and motivation. And, of course, all the general physical and mental wellbeing perks described earlier still stand, which roughly translate to reduced sick leave and happier, healthier staff.

Lots of inland waterway organisations offer corporate volunteering, but a stand-out initiative is **'plastic fishing'** (*Top Right*) on the Thames with environmental charity Hubbub. Your team will be taken out in one of a fleet of punts made from 99 per cent recycled plastic waste from the river. Each time the boats go 'fishing', volunteers collect more bottles from the Docklands, which are then recycled to make more punts. 'It's the ultimate example',

CRT's towpath orchard will ultimately stretch 80km (50 miles) along West Midlands waterways.

the organisation says, 'of the circular economy in action.'

Workplaces should also consider the Canal & River Trust's **adoption** scheme, whereby an organisation (it doesn't have to be corporate – other affiliated groups like parish councils or watersports clubs are welcome) commits to maintaining a stretch of waterway or creating a new green space for the whole community to enjoy.

Finally, give a thought to saving lives on our inland waterways by volunteering for the **RNLI** (*Above*). Although most people think of it as a coastal charity, 5 per cent of all launches take place on the Thames, and Tower lifeboat station,

● (Top) *Plastic fishing can be a fun way to get afloat and make a difference.*

(Above) *RNLI's busiest lifeboat station is inland, in London.*

which operates in central London, is the organisation's busiest. It opened in 2002 and has launched over 8,350 times, rescuing almost 2,000 people and saving 334 lives in that time. The crew at Tower – which is made up of 55 volunteers and ten full-timers – man the station in 12-hour shifts and are ready to launch within 90 seconds every day of the year. As well as lifeboat crew, RNLI also regularly appeals for volunteers to fill other roles, from press officers to fundraisers to shop volunteers.

Among the most popular waterways volunteering roles is that of lock-keeper, and one place where they're put to good use is at Hillmorton on the Oxford Canal.

Locks 2 & 3 here are, according to the Canal & River Trust's Annual Lockage Report 2021, the busiest in the country. As such, a ten-strong band of volunteers comes in handy between April and October each year with, typically, two on duty each day.

The group is led by husband-and-wife team Kevin and Taryn, who started helping out ten years ago. Despite the constant flow of boats (anything up to 100 or more a day during peak season), they're quick to point out that the role isn't limited to heaving open lock gates. Litter picks, maintenance of the beams and paddle gear, and gardening are among other site duties. Crucially, they also walk the flight at the start of each day to check all is in order before the boats start coming through.

Taryn is one of only two ladies on the Hillmorton team, and is keen to see more women consider the role. The group is made up of people from all walks of life, from accountants and engineers to postmen and paramedics, bringing a diverse range of skills and experiences. The couple say that lock-keeping provides a good amount of moderate exercise, and the social interaction with boaters and the public helps stimulate the brain. The varied nature of the role means no two days are ever the same.

Classroom-based training is given on the use of lifejackets, water rescue, first aid and safe operation of locks. Following the formal training and a period of supervised practical experience, volunteers will take a competency assessment before becoming a fully fledged lock-keeper. They typically give at least one day a week during the high season.

☛ canalrivertrust.org.uk/volunteer

● *Make friends and learn new skills while restoring waterways heritage.*

Canal restoration is a rich seam of volunteering opportunities for people looking to bring more miles of our inland waterways back into navigation after decades of dereliction. It's worth finding out if there's a long-lost stretch in your local area and getting in touch with the designated society spearheading its renaissance.

Alternatively, sign up for a week-long 'canal camp' (aka working holiday) with the Waterway Recovery Group, a subsidiary of the Inland Waterways Association. WRG has led some of the UK canal network's most ambitious restoration projects in the last 50 years, many of which have come to fruition and opened up routes that are common cruising grounds to today's boaters, and well loved by towpath users too.

It started life as a merry band of canal enthusiasts with nothing more than a couple of shovels and a can-do attitude; these days it's a slick operation giving people of all ages and from all walks of life a taste of building bridges, restoring lock chambers, operating excavators and laying bricks. You'll find Duke of Edinburgh's Award participants rubbing shoulders with seasoned waterway enthusiasts, and skilled engineers standing alongside complete novices.

The working day usually runs from 9am to 5pm (depending on the weather), with plenty of tea breaks and lunch on site. In the evening, there's a home-cooked meal and time to put your feet up. You'll also be able to join organised social activities (visits to local attractions, cinema trips etc) if you want to.

Volunteers on WRG working holidays must be aged over 18 but previous experience is not required. A week's holiday costs £70, including all meals, basic accommodation (usually in a village hall or scout hut), transport from the nearest station, as well as 'lots of laughter, mud and fun'.

Over the years I've interviewed a number of people who have taken part in these holidays and they give glowing testimonials. One repeat customer reported: 'I get to meet people I would never normally cross paths with, do things that others like me never do, and who knows, I've started so young that I might see a fully operational canal pass through some locks I've restored eventually.' Another young woman explained how her involvement with WRG 'taught me to be unapologetic about having an "unusual" interest, which is a very valuable life lesson'.

WRG also offers family camps, with more child-friendly activities such as bird-box making and vegetation clearance on the itinerary. These weekend breaks accommodate kids aged from 6 to 14 years old. They cost £15 and include all meals, accommodation (families will be sleeping in private facilities as family units throughout the weekend) and evening activities.

☛ waterways.org.uk/waterways/sites/waterway-recovery-group

Learn new skills while restoring waterways heritage on a WRG Canal Camp.

Case study

MIKE GILHAM, VOLUNTEER DECK HAND ON THE *JOHN BUNYAN* COMMUNITY BOAT, BEDFORD & MILTON KEYNES WATERWAY TRUST

I've never had a boat of my own, but I've always been interested in boats. At one stage we considered buying a narrowboat, but my wife developed mobility problems so that became out of the question. One Sunday we had a cream tea aboard the *John Bunyan* community boat and my wife noticed that they were looking for volunteers. Having retired, I thought it would be a nice way to fill my time.

I've come in at a basic level – as deck hand – but the aim is to one day steer the boat. It's 72ft long and 10ft 6in wide, so pretty big! We just about manage to scrape into the locks and when we cruise down to Kempston, where the river is really narrow and winding, it's like something out of *The African Queen*. It's a real adrenaline rush.

My role is to sit at the front of the boat on the way out, telling the skipper via radio how close he is to the bank or if the navigation is clear. It's a brilliant job; listening to the water, enjoying the view and being served the occasional cup of tea from the cabin crew inside.

On the way back I swap with the other deck hand at the stern of the boat, by the skipper. You start to see how he or she controls the boat, which is something I really want to do. I keep asking: 'Can I have a go?' When there aren't passengers aboard, I'm sometimes allowed. Last year I actually took the boat off the mooring in the marina and cruised into Bedford.

The boat does about 170 cruises a season and all the profits go to the Bedford & Milton Keynes Waterway Trust for the development of a 26km new waterway park, which will link the River Great Ouse in Bedford to the Grand Union Canal in Milton Keynes. The boat is run entirely by volunteers and they're such a mix of people and ages – from teens to retirees like me, medical reps to former pilots. That's been a big draw. Being my age, in my 60s, and mixing with people in their 20s and 30s again and feeling part of that group is tremendous. It's a real breath of fresh air.

Like everyone, I have days when I think, 'Oh, I've had enough.' But then I drive down to the boat, get my kit out of the car, have a quick chat with the rest of the crew, and by the time I'm sailing out of the marina I'm already starting to switch off and relax. Where else can you spend a fantastic afternoon on the river, with people you like, making others happy?

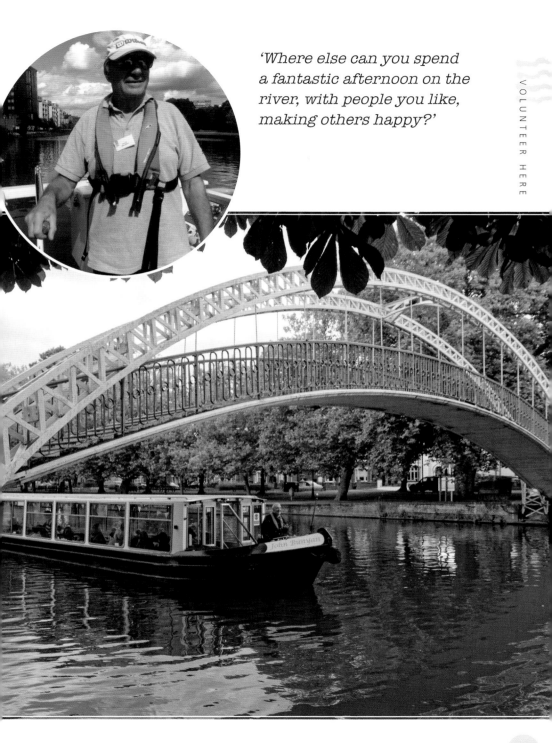

'Where else can you spend
a fantastic afternoon on the
river, with people you like,
making others happy?'

ON YOUR
BIKE

12

Cycling our waterways requires courtesy
but the rewards are huge, whether
that's on a 'hydrobike', pedalo or with
two wheels firmly on the towpath

There is a wonderful social history blog called The Victorian Cyclist (it later spawned a book called *Revolution: How the Bicycle Reinvented Modern Britain*), which charts the joys and perils of cycling in the late 19th century. Likely you'll dip into it expecting tales of extravagantly moustachioed men astride penny-farthings, or bloomer-clad women breathlessly describing their first taste of emancipation on two wheels. But what is more striking is that the things that made bicycling suddenly so popular back then are still pertinent today: an easy escape to the countryside for city dwellers, holiday opportunities both at home and abroad, assorted mental and physical wellbeing boons.

In 1896, Arthur Conan Doyle publicly endorsed this new obsession in *Scientific American*. 'When the spirits are low,' he is quoted, 'when the day appears dark, when work becomes monotonous, when hope hardly seems worth having, just mount a bicycle and go out for a spin … without thought on anything but the ride you are taking.'

It's a treatment many people self-prescribed during the torpor of pandemic lockdowns, when sales of bicycles soared to such an extent there became a global shortage. More free time, quieter roads, a demand for socially distanced travel and general wanderlust after months confined to our homes made us just as bicycle crazy as our Victorian forebears.

A question of speed

Our blue corridors proved particularly popular places to get back in the saddle or to try the sport for the first time. As with jogging, the relatively flat gradient makes it a great place to build up fitness, and there have been huge strides in upgrading towpath surfaces in recent years to make them more accessible to cyclists. But unlike cycle lanes on city streets, it's important to remember that our canal, river and lake paths are multi-use spaces. As such, waterways cycling comes with a caveat, especially on our increasingly congested urban towpaths: if you're looking to race or commute in a mad rush, this isn't the place to do it.

Indeed, speed has become such a sore point on certain stretches of our inland waterways that in 2021 the Canal & River Trust trialled a new speed awareness device in the West Midlands to encourage cyclists to be considerate and slow down. It worked by detecting the speed of cyclists as they approached, flashing a 'Thank you' if they were cycling at a leisurely pace, or the words #StayKindSlowDown if they were going too fast. Although there isn't an official speed limit for cycling along the towpath, the trial devices were set so that anyone cycling below 8mph (dubbed 'the considerate speed') got the green light. In instances where the towpath narrows, said CRT, this speed may be less.

Gavin Passmore, the charity's community engagement manager, said: 'We're asking cyclists to be sensible and to think about where they are and the people around them. Those on foot, including boaters accessing the water, have priority on our towpaths and, quite simply, those on bikes who need or want to travel quickly should use a route away from the canal. On busy stretches of canals or where the towpath is narrow, the safest option may be to get off your bike and walk.'

Towpaths are for everyone so stick to a considerate speed and be prepared to give way to pedestrians.

While speed is the main issue when it comes to considerate biking on our towpaths, it isn't the only one. The Inland Waterways Association has a useful 'Cycling Code' providing other prompts to better share the space.

- Slow down when approaching anglers, towpath walkers and other towpath users, especially family groups and disabled people or those with reduced mobility, and be prepared to dismount or wait for people to get out of your way.

- Always have a bell or horn fitted to your cycle and ALWAYS use it when approaching other users of the towpath.

- Be prepared to dismount when local signs or common sense indicate that you should, for example at congested locations and under low, narrow or blind bridges.

- Be considerate to all other users of the towpath. Pedestrians have priority. Be particularly aware of boat crews operating locks or bridges or stepping off a boat on to the towpath.

- Slow down when approaching bridges, locks and other structures, especially when there is a blind bend and you cannot see who or what is ahead of you, and be prepared to stop.

- Be aware that very occasionally a towpath crosses a road, for example when there is no room under a road bridge for a towpath. Be prepared to stop and be aware of fast-moving traffic on busy main roads.

- Watch out for hazards on the towpath such as ropes from boats, mooring stakes and bollards. Allow anglers time to move their tackle before you try to pass.

- If cycling at night, have lights fitted to your cycle and use them.

- Wearing headphones can limit communication between cyclist and other users. For this reason it is not recommended.

- Avoid cycling in large groups or having races with fellow cyclists – the towpaths are not an appropriate place for this.

- Be friendly to other waterway users. The towpaths are there for everyone to enjoy.

What sort of bike?

The ideal bicycle for your waterways ride really depends on the terrain. Unless you want tingling wrists from bouncing around on ruts and potholes or, worse, to be thrown off into the water, it's worth checking out the state of the towpath beforehand. Don't assume that just because a waterside stretch is tarmacked through a busy town, it will be like that for its entire length.

Unfortunately, popular routing apps like Google Maps won't get you very far with surface queries, so it's worth asking on cycling forums first, or plotting your route on either Komoot (komoot.com/) or Cycle.Travel (cycle.travel/). The first promises to tailor your journey to the type of bike you're riding, whether that's a beefy mountain one or a rather more delicate road bike, using topographic routing. The excellent Cycle.Travel, meanwhile, claims to 'analyse the base map data in more depth than any other site'. It says that thousands of lines of code assess surface quality, access restrictions and junction layouts to calculate the best route. The algorithms also take into account landforms and features to prioritise scenic routes, including waterways ones, and to avoid your ride being blighted by busy roads.

When it comes to tyres, hybrid tyres or a thinner mountain tyre should suffice beside most canals, rivers and lakes, giving a smooth ride on harder paths and enough grip when the going gets tough. Oversized off-road tyres are not only unnecessary in the main, but on sodden towpaths they can actually do damage by churning up the mud. Talking of which, mudguards are a sensible feature on any waterways bike, not only to stop the gears and brakes getting clogged up and to keep your lights relatively clear, but to prevent unsightly smatterings on your clothes too.

Navigation authorities generally do a good job at cutting back vegetation, but you're still likely to ride over thorns and branches and potentially pick up

a puncture. Invest in self-sealing inner tubes, tyre liners or, best, puncture-resistant tyres. Always carry a pump, basic tools and a spare inner tube or a puncture repair kit if you can.

If you're planning on taking an electric bike out to explore the inland waterways, they must meet the following criteria to have the same legal standing as regular non-assisted bicycles and to be allowed on bike paths (including towpaths):

* Electric assistance can only be provided to a maximum of 25km/h (15.5mph)
* The motor used must be of no more than 250 watts (maximum continuous rated power)
* The e-bike's pedals must be in motion for motor assistance to be provided
* The rider must be 14 years old or over

Planning your route

Komoot and Cycle.Travel have already been covered and are excellent resources for planning a waterside cycle. However, it's worth checking out the Canal & River Trust's route recommendations too (canalrivertrust.org.uk/enjoy-the-waterways/cycling/canal-cycling-routes), and obviously Sustrans (sustrans.org.uk), which is custodian of the National Cycle Network.

Although it might be tempting to prioritise rural canal rides, these can sometimes be the very worst surfaces to cycle on. The Shropshire Union, for

● *The Way of the Roses loosely follows the River Lune and the River Wenning into the Pennines, before taking in other rivers later in the route.*

example, is a favourite among boaters for its atmospheric cuttings, but try traversing them on two wheels and you'll likely find the water draining down to the towpath has made it a veritable quagmire in places.

River paths, by and large, have more challenging surfaces and often come with obstacles like stiles to negotiate. There's also the issue of access, as many go through private property. Where it is possible to follow them, however, rivers can make for lovely two-wheeled trips, and following one from its source can add a pleasing narrative to the ride.

Unfortunately, Britain doesn't have an equal to the long-distance river routes of the Loire, Rhône, Danube et al on the Continent, with extremely cycle-friendly paths running alongside and plentiful camping opportunities, but don't dismiss a bike holiday in Blighty out of hand. You might just have to be a bit more creative and allow your waterways fix to be necessarily fragmented rather than a long, continuous theme. Consider, for example, the **Devon Coast to Coast**, from Ilfracombe on the north coast to Plymouth on the south, which combines beaches and estuaries with the lush green valleys of West Country rivers. Up north, the **Way of the Roses** (*Above*), which stretches 274km (170 miles) between Morecambe and Bridlington, also incorporates periodic waterway elements as it traverses the Lune Valley and Yorkshire Dales.

For long-distance riding, the best tip

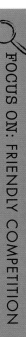

FOCUS ON: FRIENDLY COMPETITION

If slowing down on a bike is anathema to you, there is one towpath in Britain where you're allowed to pick up some pace – at least, for one day only. The Montgomery Canal Triathlon is organised annually in aid of the ongoing restoration of that waterway. It is one of the most popular cross-border events, starting in Newtown in Wales and ending in Shropshire.

The event challenges participants to cycle, walk and canoe the 56km (35-mile) length of the canal in one day. Starting in Newtown, the original destination of the canal, entrants usually cycle 27km (17 miles) to Welshpool along resurfaced towpath. After this, it's 18km (11 miles) on foot to Morton, followed by a 11km (7-mile) canoe to the Weston Arm, Lower Frankton. Note that the distance can (and does) change, depending on restoration work being carried out. This laid-back event is a lovely day out for families with children, as well as experienced triathletes.

is to travel light and build up your fitness beforehand, even if you're planning to take it slow. And although you can't control our notoriously unpredictable weather, you can factor in Plan Bs – by which I mean keep your schedule fairly flexible to allow for lazy mornings in a coffee shop to wait out rain showers. If you're planning to book accommodation ahead, only do so for a couple of nights in advance for this very reason. It will give you leeway to leave your bike chained up in inclement conditions, rather than feeling pressure to keep moving to make the next stop.

Finally, on the subject of accommodation, it's always worth checking what the security arrangements are for your bike. Some hotel chains, for example, will let you bring it into your room for peace of mind overnight.

HEALTHY HEARTS

Although all exercise is healthy, cycling is particularly good for you. If you're working out at the gym or in a pool, you tend to call it a day after 30 minutes to an hour. But when it comes to being on a bike by water, we're generally prepared for a long haul – anything up to two to three hours or more. Exercising for extended periods of time is good for the heart, expanding its capacity and strength.

Pedal boats and hydrocycles

Of course, you don't have to limit yourself to cycling beside the water – pedalling on it is just as viable an adventure. It doesn't have to be in a boxy pedalo either (although you'll find plenty of boating lakes across the country offering these for hire), for modern 'hydrocycles' boast stylish design and precision engineering. A few years ago I trialled one of the newest offerings, the Schiller Water Bike, on the River Leam. It has a robust 6cm- (2in)-wide frame set in a futuristic lightning-bolt shape, and takes about 10 minutes to assemble. Step aboard and the bike barely wobbles – indeed, so stable was the platform that the rep pointed out where an additional front deck could be laid for yoga. Manoeuvrability was similarly impressive (although you're best keeping to deep, weed-free waters) and Schiller claims you can reach not-to-be-sniffed-at speeds of over 10mph.

At roughly £3,500 a pop, they're probably not going to be overcrowding our lakes and reservoirs any time soon. A cheaper option might be to hire a hydrobike and there are few more scenic spots than **Lower Lough Erne**. Castle Archdale Boat Hire and Watersports at Irvinestown rents them for £20 for the hour, and you can even take your dog or, for an additional £5 child seat hire, youngsters too.

In recent years there have been a couple of notable river expeditions on floating bikes or pedal-powered boats including Dhruv Boruah, who cycled the length of the Thames on a bamboo bicycle fixed to two yellow floats, with a rudder and pedal-powered propeller at the front. With a fishing net hooked on either side, he collected plastic litter along the way to generate awareness of pollution. A couple of years later, veteran adventurer Jason Lewis also used pedal power to make an environmental point, taking a hand-built 8-metre (26-foot) pedal boat on a 1,207km (750-mile) trip around Wales and documenting examples of sustainable living as he did so.

But my favourite example of 'cycling' on water is the sadly now defunct Dad's Boats enterprise at Ludham on the Norfolk Broads. Until 2022, the company was selling extraordinarily beautiful pedal-powered, dinghy-sized craft. These two-person vessels, in which the boaters face each other as they propel it, took their form from a single-seater pedal boat that David Williams (the 'Dad' of the company) built from plywood and an old hand drill on his parents' dining room table aged 16. He called it 'The Sieve', for it leaked badly. Then it languished in the garden while he went off to do National Service. On his return it had deteriorated so much it was broken up for firewood. Yet the prototype sparked a lifetime of experimentation and adventure on pedal boats, including a model called the Cyclone, which carried his wife on their honeymoon around the Norfolk Broads and his good friend on a 12½-hour circumnavigation of the Isle of Wight. While the company has now ceased production, you can still hire their boats on the **Thames at Cliveden** (boatingatcliveden.co.uk) for £35 p/h, on the **Monmouthshire & Brecon Canal** from Beacon Park Boats (beaconparkdayboats.co.uk) from £30 per day, and at home on the **Broads** through Hippersons (hippersons.co.uk) for £75 for half a day or £100 for a full day.

Pedalos offer a good workout on water.

Case study

RICHARD FAIRHURST, EDITOR OF *CYCLE.TRAVEL* AND
SUSTRANS VOLUNTEER

Cycling is all about pace. There are riders who strive continuously to improve theirs, fixated on an Apple Watch readout or a Garmin mounted on the handlebar stem. There are those who log 'personal bests'. There are those who possessively guard their segment times on Strava, training for the day that another cyclist bests their hill-climb by half a second.

That's pretty much the antithesis of waterways cycling. Yet towpath riding, too, is about pace. It's faster than boating or walking; you cover more ground. Yet it's still slow enough to slip into the canal mindset. With cobbles to bump over, dogs to dodge, and the perennial time-sapping danger of tempting waterside pubs, you're hardly at risk of hitting Tour de France sprint speeds.

I've boated the tough Pennine canals, the Huddersfield Narrow and the Rochdale. I loved them both: the industrial heritage, the bohemian air of Hebden Bridge and Todmorden, the urban edge of Ancoats and Ashton. It's a good ten days' work with a fit crew. On a bike, you can cover them in two, three days, yet you're still engaging fully with canal life. You stop to chat with boaters, nod appreciatively as anglers lumber their poles aside, offer up a 'good dog' as dog-walkers draw up the leash.

And then there's a whole secret network open to cyclists – the as yet unrestored canals, forgotten in the 50s, silted and obstructed but still with a working towpath. The little-known Crumlin Arm, a Little Switzerland in South Wales, a mountainside waterway not yet open to boats. The 'Northern Reaches' of the Lancaster Canal, the Lake District's own canal. The gorgeous Montgomery in mid-Wales, navigable only in places, but rideable from top to toe.

You'll look out of place on a carbon-fibre road bike. Bring your simplest steed: a 90s mountain bike, a rusty old Raleigh, a practical but unglamorous Decathlon. Leave your tyres a little bit flat to cushion against cobbles and tree roots. Draw up an unambitious schedule, and expect to fail it. It's all about pace, you see. Just not in the way the Strava-ites would have it.

'Bring your simplest steed'

WHERE IT'S AT...

BRITAIN'S BEST WATERWAYS RIDES

St Matthew's Church on the shore of Rutland Water.

✳ Rutland Water

(*Above*) Although England's largest reservoir by surface area, Rutland Water is more than manageable for cycling newbies looking for a waterways day out. The 24km (15-mile) circular ride, starting from Oakham, can be extended by a 9.6km (6-mile) out-and-back along the Hambleton peninsula. The route covers mixed terrain and has a few hills, but nothing too severe. Cycle hire is available.

✳ Ulster Canal

The Ulster Canal Trail is a 77km (48-mile) cycle route between Maghery, Co Armagh and Clones, Co Monaghan, taking in some stunning lowland lakes and rivers. There are plenty of pub stops along the way, and sightseeing opportunities at historic houses and characterful towns and villages.

✳ Kennet & Avon Canal

The 132km (82-mile) Kennet & Avon Canal route will necessitate a few selfie stops, notably in front of Bradford on Avon's Tithe Barn, the Pewsey White Horse, the mammoth flight of locks at Caen Hill and elegant Dundas Aqueduct. Starting in Reading (to finish in Bath) is best, as you can book in for a restorative soak at Thermae Bath Spa afterwards. If you're looking for something you can do in a day, try the 35km (22-mile) stretch between Bath and Devizes.

✳ Loch Leven

This flat, circular ride around beautiful Loch Leven in central Scotland is just 21km (13 miles) long but packs in a lot of wildlife (osprey, kingfishers, otters), plus views out to Lochleven Castle on one of the islands, where Mary, Queen of Scots was imprisoned in 1567. There are café stops along the way, so you can stretch out your cycle in this glorious national nature reserve a little longer.

✱ Peregrine Path

Straddling the border between England and Wales and winding alongside the River Wye, this 12km (7.5-mile) route is a superb family ride. You'll start in the historic market town of Monmouth, before taking in the huge Wye Gorge to Symonds Yat. Keep your eyes peeled for the peregrine falcons launching from the limestone outcrops above.

✱ Taff Trail

The route runs for 88km (55 miles) between Cardiff and Brecon along a mixture of riverside trails, railway paths and forest roads. Tackle it on a sturdy bike to make sure you're covered for every surface, and enjoy, especially, the Merthyr section. Cefn-coed Viaduct, the third-largest viaduct in Wales, is a particular highlight, offering cyclists a marvellous view of the Taff Fawr as it rushes through the valley.

✱ Swale Trail

This is one for aspiring mountain bikers, including children, with around 70 per cent of the 19km (12-mile) Yorkshire Dales route from Reeth to Keld on unsurfaced tracks, while the rest follows quiet back roads. Your waterways interest comes in the form of the River Swale – the trail snakes beside it. Look out for Keld's wonderful waterfalls as you near the end.

✱ Crinan Canal

(*Below*) We've saved the best for last. This short (14.5km/9 miles), utterly gorgeous Scottish waterway linking Ardrishaig on Loch Fyne with Crinan on the west coast is best tackled in late spring when dolphins can sometimes be seen from the Crinan end. The canal was built to let boats journeying from the Clyde to the sea cut more than 160km (100 miles) off their voyage, and has been described as the most beautiful shortcut in Britain. There's good reason – the countryside is stunning and varied (from bogland to lush banks of grasses and reeds), and the whole route is blissfully flat and runs along well-surfaced towpath, with one very quiet road section.

A cyclist passing Bannatyne Cottage near Cairnbaan on the Crinan Canal.

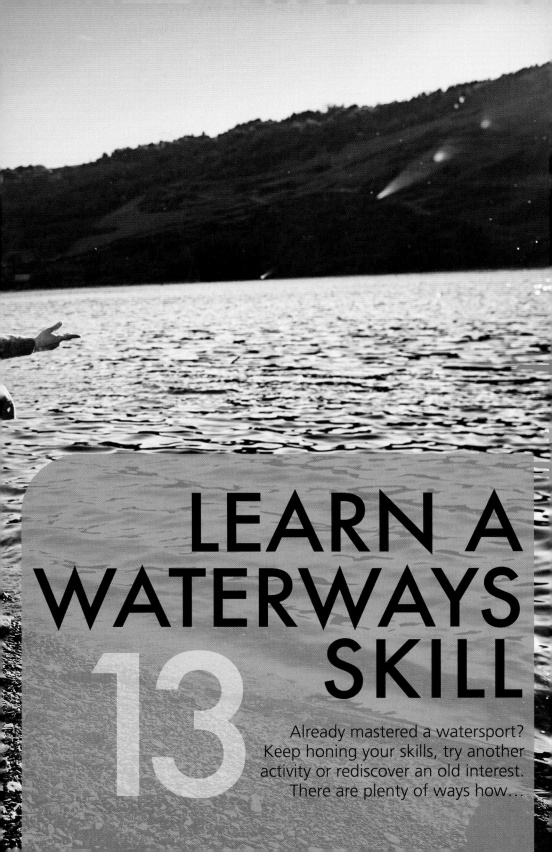

LEARN A WATERWAYS SKILL

13

Already mastered a watersport?
Keep honing your skills, try another
activity or rediscover an old interest.
There are plenty of ways how…

Career-wise, we're living in what's known as the multi-hyphen era, with almost everyone admitting they've a side hustle or even an entire portfolio of other jobs. Being called a jack-of-all-trades used to carry a whiff of condescension – these days, we're no one if we're not juggling at least a dozen different interests and skills.

The multi-hyphen mentality can equally be applied to the inland waterways, I think, and help us glean even more enjoyment from the rivers, lakes and canals we frequent. When I started canal boating, I was simply that – a canal boater. But a series of courses, exams, informal chats, demonstrations, YouTube videos and mugging up with books over the years has turned me into a certified helmsman/semi-competent coracle builder/beginner gansey knitter/all-but-forgotten fender-maker/seasick Channel-crosser/waterways journalist, among other slashes.

Far from feeling I've spread myself too thin, constantly learning about the boats, traditions and navigations I encounter has helped consolidate the one thing I've known all along – that I love our waterways. Chipping away at the topic from different angles simply makes it shine more brilliantly, rather like cutting a diamond.

Learning is good for us in multiple other ways too. Picking up a new skill, on a very basic level, helps us feel better about ourselves. It builds self-esteem and gives us the confidence to achieve other goals or overcome difficulties in our daily lives. Just as importantly, learning from local or online experts, attending courses, or going along to an educational talk can connect us with other like-minded people and provide a sense of belonging, of feeling valued and accepted. This affirmation of self-worth can have enormous wellbeing benefits.

And let's not forget the sense of purpose that learning fosters. It gives us a goal to work towards, the feeling of things moving forward and a focus that can often take our minds away from

It's a small world: Model boat building can be a great hobby to revisit as an adult.

other stresses that might be bothering us. It's surely the reason the pandemic saw such a spike in people turning to language-learning, or mastering an instrument, or honing other hobbies and creative skills. Our canals and rivers weren't exempt from this craze. I remember the editorial focus at *Waterways World* magazine moving away from the usual travelogues and cruising advice to information on such disparate subjects as online resources for tracing canal ancestry, DIY boat projects that can be completed in the garden shed, or how to swot for a Marine Radio Short Range Certificate.

It wasn't all about learning something new, either. Many waterways enthusiasts used the time to rediscover an old interest. Lindsey Amrani, editor of *Model Boats* magazine, reported 'a noticeable increase' in people taking up the hobby after Covid hit, with working vessels (tugs, barges etc) proving especially popular. One model-boater I spoke to at the time said the crisis had compelled him to revisit an idyllic hire holiday he'd taken with classmates on the day they'd finished school, decades before, by making an exact replica of the boat they'd rented. He couldn't

● *Raft-making is a perennially popular team-building activity.*

explain this 'strange choice', he said, but Hornby's chief executive Lyndon Davies probably got near the nub of it when commenting on his own company's pandemic boom to the *Guardian* in 2020, insisting the hobby provided both comfort and amusement in times of national crisis.

Messing about in boats

If you're looking to make a full-scale boat and set sail in it yourself, there are plenty of great courses offering instruction on everything from basic raft-making to more sophisticated stitch-and-glue canoes and dinghies.

Black Mountain Adventure in Brecon (blackmountain.co.uk/tours/raft-building) promises plain fun as well as edification in its 2–3-hour group course building a raft and putting it to the test afterwards on the River Wye. You'll be equipped with buoyancy aids, helmets and paddles, and given a short

177

If your woodworking skills are up to it, have a go at building your own boat.

time to design your raft before the construction and competition element ensues. The activity is aimed at everyone from families and birthday groups to companies looking to give their staff a novel team-building treat. The minimum group size is eight, and prices are from £32pp.

If you'd rather do it in your back garden, there's a lovely set of instructions online for how to build a plastic **milk bottle raft** (instructables.com/Build-a-Milk-Jug-Raft/). The project carries virtually no cost, and can be completed by anyone who knows how to use a drill and basic hand tools. Just be warned that, depending on how much milk you get through at home, it could take a few months to save the necessary number of bottles from your recycling bin (although any other sturdy drinks container will do).

For something a little more robust, have a go at building a boat from a kit. **Fyne Boat Kits** in Cumbria (fyneboatkits.co.uk) offers a huge range of projects, from canoes, kayaks and rowing boats to surf and paddleboards. I'm rather fond of their 'Dinky Dory'

3.6-metre (12-foot) clinker-style rowing boat, which can carry a large payload (200kg/450lb) but is still cartoppable. The draught is only about 100mm (4in), making it ideal for exploring shallow water. The company maintains it can be assembled in about 40 hours from the kit, priced £1,200, using very few tools and basic woodworking skills. There's obviously a comprehensive building manual provided in the kit, but you're also paying for technical support from a competent builder by phone or email if necessary. If you like the idea but don't feel confident in your woodworking skills, you could always sign up for one of the firm's courses, which span either five or ten days. Check its website for dates and further details.

For a quicker build, you can **make a coracle** – a traditional one-person, woven-wood boat – in a single weekend. Expect to pay around £350, which will include all materials, instruction and possibly lunch too,

● *Do you know your bowline from your clove hitch? There's a course for that…*

with details of different providers on The Coracle Society's website: coraclesociety. org.uk. You'll also find instructions to build your own at home. When I tried one of these courses a few years ago, in south Oxfordshire, the whole group was given a quick boating lesson on the Thames at Wallingford afterwards. Granted, this mainly saw me lazily spinning into tangles of overhanging willow tree, but it was also a good reminder of how different a familiar patch of river can look when you take to the water in a new craft or activity. By shifting off the bench seat on to the very bottom of the coracle, for example, I could follow our instructor under the lowest, overgrown arch of Wallingford Bridge to see the tiny flowers growing from the cracked brickwork and hear the strange sound our voices made bouncing off the low ceiling. A perfect grotto, this secret Thames seemed a million miles from the open water I'd cruised down on my narrowboat.

Perhaps you'd rather learn to better control a boat before building one yourself, in which case an **Inland Waterways Helmsman's Course** could be more suited. It assumes no prior knowledge and so is ideal for the first timer, but even experienced narrowboat and cruiser captains can learn a thing or two to make their boating safer and more enjoyable. Courses take place over two days and can be taken either on a centre's boat or your own. Find a list of providers on the Royal Yachting Association's website (rya.org.uk).

Meanwhile, if you're a boatowner looking to take on more maintenance work rather than relying on professional boatyards, take a look at **River Canal Rescue**'s (rivercanalrescue.co.uk) handy courses, which usually run over a weekend and are designed to help you become more familiar with the engine, electrics and plumbing of your craft.

Remember, though, that upskilling doesn't have to mean achieving a formal qualification. If you're looking to improve your general boating you could always just learn some **useful knots** instead, or pick up some **steering tips** by watching online instructional videos.

Conservation classes

If you're not so much interested in getting afloat as discovering more about the waterways generally, there are plenty of resources to scaffold your learning. Tristan Gooley's excellent book *How to Read Water* is a fine place to start. Anyone who spends time in, on or by the water, whether sailing in the Lakes or simply playing Poohsticks with grandkids, will benefit from some of the extraordinary insights. Learn, for instance, how prone the rivers you navigate are to flash flooding based on the shape of the bridges that span them, or what towpath puddles can reveal about the animals living alongside our waterways, the habits of the walkers who trudge these routes regularly, prevailing winds and the direction of the sun.

Those looking to take an active role in protecting our rivers, lakes and canals, meanwhile, could do worse than signing up for environmental charity Thames21's flagship training course, **Leading Action for Healthy Rivers** (thames21. org.uk). It promises to teach everything you need to plan and run safe, effective, enjoyable waterway improvement events as well as champion healthy rivers. You will learn about the challenges faced by urban rivers, and be able to identify what tasks a group of volunteers can do, which will really make a difference, plus find out more about leadership responsibilities and the health and safety implications of working in and near water.

Staying on the conservation theme, **Canal & River Trust's Open Days**, (*Below*) whereby members of the public are invited to see maintenance and heritage tasks up close, are a great way to learn more about the colossal effort waterways custodians make to keep our navigations ticking along nicely. They take place across the country and encompass a variety of sites, work and slightly unnerving experiences (you can't stand at the bottom of a drained lock on the Hatton Flight in Warwickshire, for example, without wondering at least once how securely all that water's being held back). I highly recommend

● *A CRT open day at Newark on the River Trent.*

them. Something staider, but no less educational, is the programme of talks held by various waterways charities, usually over the quieter winter months, on everything from UK canal heritage to cruising reports from the Continent. Check out your local branch of the Inland Waterways Association (waterways.org. uk) or a nearby restoration society to see what's coming up.

Get crafty

For those of a creative or practical bent, learning a waterways craft can be a great way to find out more about the history of our canals and rivers, or simply save you some cash in future.

Fender-making courses are a good example of the latter: rather than forking out £25 on a side fender every time one twangs off your boat in a lock, just learn how to make them yourself. Courses are advertised periodically at various places around the canal network, and usually cost around £50 for the day. You should get all the materials and tools, plus a step-by-step tutorial through every knot, twist and turn required to keep churning

Teach yourself how to paint in the traditional roses and castles folk art style.

them out for years to come.

A less practical but certainly more evocative canal boat adornment is the painting style known as **roses and castles** (*Above*), which has its origins in our waterways' cargo-carrying past. It was prominently used on the fixed panels inside the back cabins of working boats, but also applied to portable items like water cans and stools. Although commercial carrying on the canals died out many years ago, this decorative tradition is still alive and well, and weekend courses will introduce beginners to the basics. Jane Marshall at Audlem on the Shropshire Union Canal, for example, advertises a two-day session costing £85 per person, including paints, brushes, practice boards and lunch, but you'll need to bring your own items to decorate. Courses are usually made up of people from a variety of backgrounds – some with a direct link to canals and others who just love the bright colours and patterns.
☞ day-star-theatre.co.uk

181

'It feels a little bit rebellious
to decorate and embellish'

Case study

HOLLY ROBBINS, CANAL FOLK ARTIST

I first got interested in canal art not long after buying and moving onto my narrowboat, *Devon Rose*, in 2019. I always have one or two craft projects on the go at any one time, and come from a long line of crafty women. In the past I've painted, embroidered, printed, bound books, made soaps, whittled and knitted. It just seemed right to try out roses and castles once I was living aboard, and it slotted perfectly into this new chapter of my life.

I'm self-taught, with the help of YouTube and a wonderful reference book called *Paint Roses and Castles* by Anne Young, which I'd recommend to anyone interested in trying canal art for themselves. As with any craft, it takes a little while to get to know the materials you're using and there was lots of trial and error at the beginning! I learned a lot about how to work with enamel paint by attending an online course with Joby Carter, a professional signwriter and fairground artist, during a Covid lockdown. You can't beat watching a master at work for picking up tips.

A lot of the success of this kind of folk painting is down to confidence, especially in your brush strokes. It took me about a year to be consistently making marks that looked nice to me, and then a lot of repetition to get proficient. My style is still refining and improving with every object I paint, and

I'm by no means a master of the craft yet. I still very much consider myself a hobbyist.

I mainly do it because I love the connection it gives me to the traditions of the waterways. In a world where nearly all our belongings are mass produced, it feels a little bit rebellious to decorate and embellish. It is also quite meditative, as it is a satisfying balance between creativity and making the same marks over and over. Painting all of the small brushstrokes is absorbing and repetitive. But other steps, like deciding the layout of a design on an object, take quite a lot of decision making.

If you want a cheap way to try it out, you can buy small pots of gloss enamel in a wide range of colours from Humbrol for about £2 each. I used these for a long time before investing in proper signwriting paint. Get some soft, long-bristled brushes, or find what works for you! Enamel paint will stick to most things, so pick up some cheap ceramic or metal objects from a charity shop to practise on. Folk art is meant to be accessible to all, so don't worry too much about whether you're doing it 'right' – if it looks lovely to you then that's all that matters!

☛ @dog.rose.crafts

Basics first - don't run before you can walk. Before even thinking of learning how to make a canal boatman's traditional spiderweb belt or entering for an RYA certificate in dinghy sailing, make sure you've got the waterways basics mastered.

Poohsticks

Many people think that just because the sport's named after a slow-witted teddy bear, there's nothing more to Poohsticks than choosing a place on the bridge above the fastest-flowing water. They'd be wrong.

In 2015, one Dr Rhys Morgan, director of engineering and education at the Royal Academy of Engineering, finally enlightened the world to the sophisticated science behind choosing the optimum stick for this underrated watersport. The main variables to consider, he said, were cross-sectional area (A), density (I), and the drag coefficient (Cd).

When it comes to area (A), look for a fairly thick stick. Whereas normally a large cross-sectional area decreases speed, drag is everything in this game. If more water is able to influence the trajectory of the stick, it will accelerate more quickly. So the greater the amount of stick surface in contact with the water, the better.

Similarly, a higher density (I) helps as the fastest part of the stream is below the surface. A stick that sinks slightly will be zippier than a stick that is bobbing about on the surface.

Finally, the drag coefficient (Cd) is dictated by the shape and roughness of the stick. For maximum drag, steer away from smooth sticks and look for something with bark. But be careful: Dr Morgan warns that just as dimples help *reduce* a golf ball's drag, so a certain type of roughness can make the stick 'apparently' smoother too.

So, far from being a game of luck, a considered, *tactical* choice of the Perfect Poohstick hinges on learning the following formula: PP = A x I x Cd. Memorise it well. Then apply it at any one of VisitEngland's suggestions of best bridges to play at:

✳ Sheepwash Bridge, Ashford in the Water, Derbyshire

✳ Morden Hall Park, London

✳ Heale Gardens, Salisbury, Wiltshire*

✳ Packhorse Bridge, Watendlath, Cumbria

✳ Mottisfont, Romsey, Hampshire*

✳ Little Wittenham Bridge, Abingdon, Oxfordshire

✳ Mathematical Bridge, Cambridge, Cambridgeshire*

✳ New Lower Bridge, Boscastle, Cornwall

✳ Bridge over Bourne Eau, Bourne, Lincolnshire

✳ Cantlop Bridge, Shrewsbury, Shropshire

✳ Essex Bridge, Shugborough, Staffordshire

✳ Hutton-le-Hole, Ryedale, North Yorkshire

* Entrance fee required.

Ok, this one is a little trickier to become proficient at. Practice is everything. And unlike Poohsticks, you'll need some fairly still water to do it – lakes or canals are good.

Stone skimming can get competitive when you're doing it with family and friends!

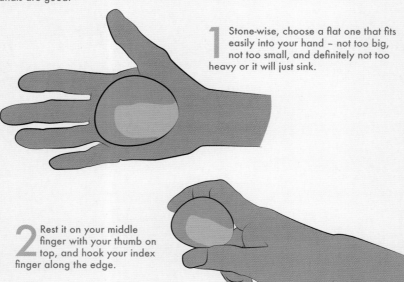

1 Stone-wise, choose a flat one that fits easily into your hand – not too big, not too small, and definitely not too heavy or it will just sink.

2 Rest it on your middle finger with your thumb on top, and hook your index finger along the edge.

186

3 Stand facing the water but at a slight angle. It sometimes helps if you duck down, so that you're already level with the water when you start your throw. Pull your arm back.

4 Give your wrist a flick as you throw, and aim out and down at the same time. Scientists reckon the best angle for the stone to enter the water is at 20 degrees.

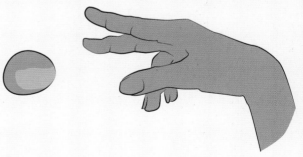

Once you've got the hang of it, stone skimming can be a real buzz. But be mindful, if you can, of the entire process – the feel of the stone in your hand before throwing, and the fading ripples it leaves behind, not just its mad, magnificent freewheeling across the water.

To learn from the best, make a beeline for the sport's annual **World Championships on Easdale Island**, near Oban in Argyll, Scotland. If you want to compete, just turn up as there are no qualifying rounds. But get there early – the maximum number of entrants is 350. For more information, including rules, visit stoneskimming.com. There's usually a Pre-Skim Party in the community hall on the evening before the competition, with a licensed bar and live music. Children are welcome.

187

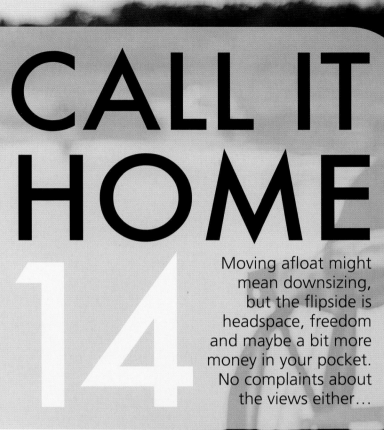

CALL IT HOME

14

Moving afloat might mean downsizing, but the flipside is headspace, freedom and maybe a bit more money in your pocket. No complaints about the views either…

For a growing number of people, our inland waterways are less a wellness 'escape' than a permanent way of life. Living afloat has exploded in popularity in the last decade, especially in cities. Canal & River Trust figures show that from 2012 to 2019, boat numbers in London grew by 84 per cent, while continuously cruising boats (those without a fixed mooring) soared by 246 per cent. It believes the majority of boats in the capital are now permanent homes.

You'll find no shortage of aspirational stories of people who have made the leap in our tabloids and broadsheets, while Instagram is full of accounts detailing boat conversions and the attractions of life that can be more or less off-grid.

Waterways living is proving a particular lure for young people, even those who aren't quite prepared to give up bricks and mortar to attain it.

● *Home is where you moor it: A growing number of people are choosing to live afloat.*

Traditionally, having a home either by or on the water was something we'd save for retirement years, but estate agents Strutt & Parker, who surveyed 2,000 people as part of their 2018 Waterside Survey, found over a quarter of under-35s and over a third of 35–39s were actively looking to live near water within five years.

When it comes to settling on a boat specifically, soaring property prices might be driving the trend, while the rise in remote working is certainly facilitating the dream. However, other reasons given for gravitating to the water often

relate to health or environmental factors. The Strutt & Parker survey found those house-hunting beside our canals, rivers and lakes were looking for relaxation (51%), better air quality (47%), views (46%), exercising opportunities (38%) and mental wellbeing (35%).

Does waterways living deliver? Well, yes, it seems to. There have been countless studies and entire books written by scientists about how and why it makes us happier. It lowers stress, boosts creativity, makes us calmer and enhances our relationships, depending on which particular report you're looking at.

Personally, I'd vouch for it too. I lived afloat for nearly five years – on my own, with a partner and eventually with a baby in tow. I've tried marina life, and being on the move; rural moorings and slap bang in the centre of London and Paris. I've tried roughing it, without even a toilet aboard, and experienced the luxury of boat life on a fully fitted liveaboard conversion too. I've loved every iteration.

Writing this four years into life on terra firma, I still miss every quirk, every quack, and will bore anyone who listens with an effusion of tales from that time – a sort of poor man's Karen Blixen, with not so much the 'I had a farm in Africa' refrain but 'I had a narrowboat on the Trent & Mersey'.

It's easy to romanticise the proximity to wildlife, the ever changing views, the feeling of having stepped out of the mainstream. But the real wellbeing boons are actually more prosaic. *Bridgerton* star Claudia Jessie, who lives on a boat in Birmingham, told *Waterways World* that for her one of the biggest draws is the small space, the sense of retreating into a shell the moment she steps aboard. Having security that isn't static – basically, home that doesn't tie her to one place – has also been good for her anxiety.

Another actress advocating liveaboard life is Nicola Thorp, who found the day-to-day slog of boat chores (everything

from emptying the loo to lighting the stove) gave her greater self-reliance 'as someone who didn't previously feel particularly useful at certain things'. In an interview, again for *Waterways World* magazine, she likened all these daily tasks that don't crop up in a regular house to little acts of boat 'self-care', which in turn reminded her to make time to service her own needs regularly too.

And then there's the much-feted community element. I wonder whether boat folk feel it more because our 'property' is on something we can never hope to own – the canal or lake or river. The waterways are 'home', but our claim to it is a shared, emotional one – and the bonds this creates are strong and satisfying. Waterways 'community' might not be evidenced as obviously as it traditionally has been on land, where churches and village halls once acted as

focal points*, but it's there all right: in the invitations to moor abreast another boat when you can't find your own space, in the offers of technical help when the water tank starts leaking, or to 'boat-sit' when you want a weekend back home with your parents. Everybody needs good neighbours – we know that from Ramsay Street days – but how lucky you are when they extend beyond the 60 feet or so of your craft to encompass the whole inland waterways network.

Do your research beforehand

If you're not 100 per cent sure whether boat life will be for you, try hiring one first. Doing so out of season will not only be cheaper, but also give you a more realistic idea of what it's like to be afloat year-round and not just in temperate summer months. It's also worth reading around the subject, or chatting to people who already live on boats.

For all the wonderful benefits I've detailed earlier, living afloat is by no

* To be fair, in London there are floating versions of both of these – a church in Hackney Wick and the roving 'Village Butty', which was created in 2015.

● *You'll need to decide whether you want to be in a marina, on a towpath mooring or continuously cruising.*

means an easy option – especially these days. In cities, where the housing crisis has played a big role in people choosing to live on boats, increasingly congested waterways are putting pressure on canal-side services such as drinking water and pump-out toilet facilities.

Permanent moorings, meanwhile, can be expensive and difficult to find and, consequently, many people are choosing to cruise continuously – which means having to move at least once every 14 days. This is fair enough if you work from home and/or have time on your hands, less so if you need to stay within commuting distance of an office, or close to local schools for your kids.

What does it cost?

If you're sure it's the right decision, the next step is to start looking for your floating home. When it comes to viewings, try and drag an experienced boater along with you – they'll be able to point out potential pitfalls and whether the craft has the full complement of fixtures and fittings to make your new life comfortable.

The cost of buying a liveaboard boat very much depends on your budget. The value of new and used craft has gone up in recent years, so for a second-hand narrowboat expect to pay about £45,000 to £50,000 and upwards of £140,000 for a new, fully fitted wide-beam boat (over 10 feet wide).

You may well find cheaper options while you're boat-hunting, but bear in mind the size of the craft and the amount of work needed to do it up. While it's perfectly possible to live on a small boat, if you don't want it to be too much of a squeeze avoid ones that are less than 15 metres (50 feet) long. At the other end of the scale, going too large (or wide) will restrict where you can travel with the boat. If you envision boat life as a constant journey of discovery around the country, you're going to come a cropper with a wide-beam on the narrow canals of the Midlands, where you simply won't fit into the locks. The ideal 'go-anywhere' size is no longer than 17 metres (57 feet) and no wider than 2 metres (6ft 10in).

Buying second-hand will almost certainly involve a survey, which can cost from £400 to £600. This in itself can often find sufficient faults to reduce the sale price by at least the same figure, but remember that you will want to follow the surveyor's advice to re-black the hull, replace sacrificial anodes etc, so make sure you've money spare after buying to complete these tasks. Allowing for other small refurbishments to make the boat 'your own' means you're probably looking to spend in the region of £1,500 post-purchase.

Licence requirements

Before moving aboard, your boat must be licensed by the authority that runs the waterway you intend to live on. In England and Wales, the majority of our inland waterways are managed by the Canal & River Trust. How much you pay for a CRT licence depends on the length and, as of 2020, the width of your boat too, and whether you want to cruise on canals and rivers, or rivers only. As an example, an 18-metre (60-foot) narrowboat annual licence for all CRT waterways will set you back in the region of £1,100, with a 10–20 per cent surcharge if your boat is wide-beam. The second-largest licensing authority is the Environment Agency, which manages the River Thames, the River Medway and a number of Eastern Counties waterways. Its charges for the River Thames relate to the length and width of your boat too, while other EA waterways charge solely by length.

To license the boat, it must first be insured. The cost will vary depending on the age and type of boat, as well as the sort of cover you want. CRT stipulates third-party insurance for at least £2m before you buy a boat licence, which will cover you for claims made against you for injury or damage if your boat

is involved in an accident. Taking out a comprehensive policy will cover your own boat, its contents and crew. The 18-metre (60-foot) narrowboat I gave as an example earlier will probably be quoted in the region of £150-plus per year.

You'll also need a valid Boat Safety Certificate (basically a boat MOT, which is carried out every four years, and will set you back another £150-ish) and your boat must have a permanent mooring that is approved by CRT. The alternative is to satisfy the Trust that you are a 'continuous cruiser'.

Moorings

Flexibility and an open mind will stand you in good stead when it comes to finding somewhere to tie up. Do not buy a boat and expect to find a residential mooring in your chosen town or city. Demand is especially high in London, the south-east, Bath and Bristol.

The cost of a mooring is difficult to predict as it depends on where it is and what facilities it offers. You can take your pick from a length of towpath (costing from £1,250 a year) to a fully serviced berth in a secure marina, which could be nearer £7,000.

Moorings on a picture-postcard canal within easy distance of London generally command more than those on less attractive and more remote waterways. Similarly, you'll pay more in a marina that offers all the bells and whistles (laundry facilities, chandlery supplies, parking, Wi-Fi etc) than you would moored up at the bottom of a farmer's field with just an extension cable connected to the nearest power point.

Before signing any mooring contract, it's important to make sure it permits

🔵 *Blacking the hull will be one of your biggest maintenance costs.*

🔵 *Living afloat with a young child has its challenges, but plenty of families make it work.*

you to live on your boat. Many providers do not offer official residential moorings and, although some will turn a blind eye if you're discreet, others are very strict on enforcing a no-liveaboard policy.

Of course, finding a permanent mooring isn't a prerequisite to living afloat. I've touched upon continuous cruising already, which can be a good option if you're genuinely looking to explore the system rather than simply 'bridge-hop' (moving short distances in a given area before returning to your starting point, ad infinitum). It's perfectly possible to combine both lifestyles – cruising while the weather's good and taking a short-term mooring in a marina or at one of CRT's winter mooring sites until spring comes around again.

Other costs

Life afloat is often sold as a cheaper alternative to renting a flat or house, and this is broadly true, but don't forget all the other bits and pieces that add up along the way. Electricity costs if you're hooked up to shore power can be higher than domestic house charges, for example, and you'll also need to budget for fuel. Most marinas in England, Scotland and Wales sell red diesel on a 60/40 split of full and lower tax rates for propulsion, and heating or power generation. In Northern Ireland, however, recreational boaters are no longer able to use red diesel for propelling their craft, and must instead buy white diesel.

If you're using gas for cooking, buying bottles is something else to factor in, as is the price of emptying your toilet's holding tank if you've got a pump-out loo aboard. The costs vary between £10 and £25 a time. Maintenance-wise, the big one is blacking your hull (basically cleaning it off and repainting), which can cost up to £1,000 (considerably cheaper if you're prepared to get your hands dirty) and is usually done every four years.

195

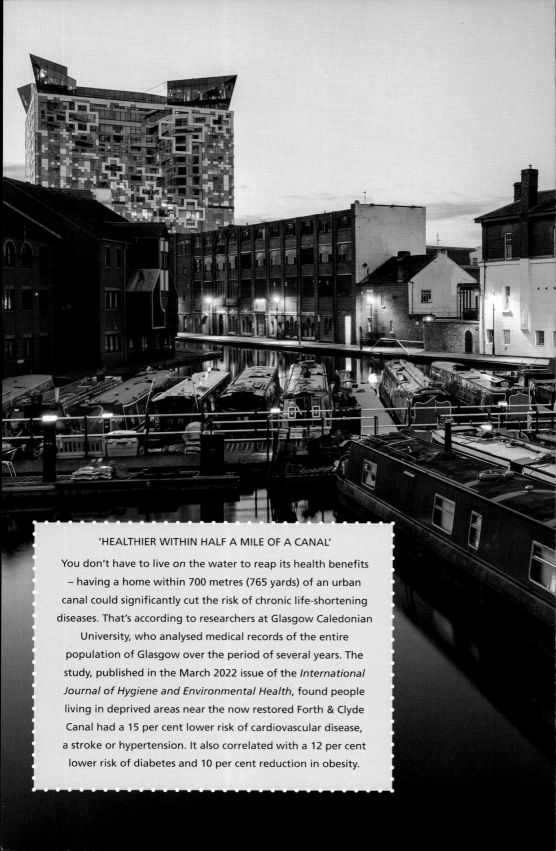

'HEALTHIER WITHIN HALF A MILE OF A CANAL'

You don't have to live *on* the water to reap its health benefits – having a home within 700 metres (765 yards) of an urban canal could significantly cut the risk of chronic life-shortening diseases. That's according to researchers at Glasgow Caledonian University, who analysed medical records of the entire population of Glasgow over the period of several years. The study, published in the March 2022 issue of the *International Journal of Hygiene and Environmental Health*, found people living in deprived areas near the now restored Forth & Clyde Canal had a 15 per cent lower risk of cardiovascular disease, a stroke or hypertension. It also correlated with a 12 per cent lower risk of diabetes and 10 per cent reduction in obesity.

Moorings in Gas Street Basin, Birmingham offer a heady mix of industrial heritage and modern redevelopment.

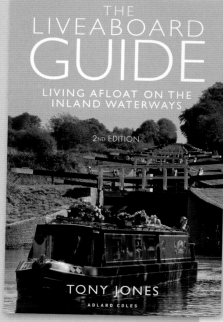

For anyone looking to move afloat, the bible is Tony Jones's *Liveaboard Guide: Living Afloat on the Inland Waterways.* It's stuffed full of details on the pleasures and practicalities, and put together by a man who really knows his stuff as Tony's been boat-dwelling for nearly 20 years. You'll find tips on choosing a boat, an assessment of the pros and cons of residential moorings versus continuous cruising, how energy consumption and power usage differs from living in a house, how to stay warm, logistical problems and – every boater's favourite topic of conversation – which loo works best. Make sure you pick up the second edition of this book (published 2019) – the updates on green boating and city living are invaluable.

For more information, plus inspiring stories of people who have made canals their home, a subscription to *Waterways World* magazine is money well spent. I know I'm biased, having worked there for many years, but it really is an excellent source of maintenance advice, cruising tips and relevant news.

For a social history of living afloat, meanwhile, look no further than Julian Dutton's *Water Gypsies*. The writer/impressionist was himself raised on a houseboat in Chelsea in the 1960s. However, his lens goes back much further, tracing a line all the way from the fisherfolk of ancient times to post-war years when floating communities became bohemian and slightly raffish, 'a place of beat poetry, bottle parties and film actors', to the current wave of young city professionals. It's an evolution from necessity to choice, Dutton notes. But he also speculates that even early boat dwellers who depended on rivers and canals for their livelihood may have shared the same 'impulse' for water, 'to occupy a place outside the stream of normal belonging'.

Finally, there are countless memoirs charting the leap from land to a new life afloat. Two of the best are Danie Couchman's *Afloat* and Helen Babbs' *Adrift*, which both draw from experiences of London's canals specifically.

TONY JONES, LIVEABOARD BOATER AND
AUTHOR OF *THE LIVEABOARD GUIDE*

I once worked out that I had moved house, on average, every eight months. I regularly lived on the road out of a rucksack for months on end, crashed at friends' houses in the spare room or on sofas, and I'd also had the occasional rental property, but I'd never really settled. I'd never felt like anywhere was 'home' enough to consider decorating.

While my vagabond lifestyle was certainly interesting and adventurous, there was always an underlying anxiety about my vulnerable housing situation, and the instability made life difficult and stressful in many other ways too. I did my best to ignore it, but I always knew I was just one stroke of bad luck away from becoming properly homeless and helpless.

I got the idea to live on a narrowboat from a friend and it seemed a perfect solution. I'd have the stability of knowing I would always have somewhere to live, while retaining the freedom to move around whenever an adventure beckoned. Plus, if you do it right, living aboard can be a relatively affordable way to live.

As soon as I moved aboard the relief was palpable. I hadn't appreciated how precarious my life had been. I remember lying in bed on my first night, my stomach fizzing with excitement and pride, knowing I was finally safe. The boat felt like sanctuary. It was my home. It was paid for. It was mine and nobody could take it away from me.

The boat provided a foundation from which I could build a life that had previously been inaccessible to me. And while life aboard isn't always a bed of roses, for someone like me it's far preferable to living in a flat enduring nightmare neighbours, or stuck in a job you hate because you have a mortgage to pay. Seventeen years later I'm still thankful for the security and stability my boat provides. I know my life could easily have turned out very differently. It would be no exaggeration to say that my boat saved me.

'I had time to become a more
loving and present mum'

Case study

HANNAH BODSWORTH, PHOTOGRAPHER AND LIVEABOARD BOATER

The boat was my way out of physical and mental burnout. I was juggling a part-time marketing job, a photography studio business, and solo parenting a four-year-old. I was underweight, working late most nights, and not getting enough sleep. My time and my finances were tight and there wasn't much room in my day for any extra obstacles. I'd reached breaking point. I didn't care if George and I lived in the tiniest of homes and cooked simple food on a camp stove, all that mattered was that I would get off the hamster wheel as soon as possible.

My eldest brother had lived on a boat for many years and helped me find a budget floating home. The relief, when we did, was immense. Moving afloat, my outgoings dropped by over £800. The inside of the boat was a tip, and we moved onto it in October when the temperature dropped below freezing, but I'd never felt such happiness. I told myself never to forget this feeling, and that everything would be okay from here. I handed in my notice on my marketing job, continuing to work part-time on my own business. I finally had the time to go inward and heal from all that had led me to that point. But most importantly, now I had time to become a more loving and present mum.

There's no doubt we've benefitted from this life, the slower existence, being immersed in nature, less material things cluttering up our lives. The boat presented new challenges – it was physically hard work and very technical – but this was a welcome trade-off to lengthy commutes, never-ending deadlines and financial stress. And the universe brought wonderful boat neighbours who were happy to show George and me the ropes. I don't know where we would have ended up without our beautiful little boat and the lovely people who have helped us to set sail. ☞ @narrowboatmama

15
FEED THE DUCKS

On the wall, at Stanford, and bobbing about in the water – ducks can tell us a lot about how we feel

If I only had a few moments left on Earth, I would kiss my family – and throw bread to the ducks. I am unreasonably fond of ducks. I wouldn't say obsessed, per se, but it's true that I write this sitting under a GREAT duck poster, and sipping tea from a duck mug. The mug I am especially fond of. It was painted by a friend to immortalise a perfect evening beside the Cromford Canal in Derbyshire when we watched the mallards, ate chips, wondered what to do about everything, and wondered nothing. Ducks can have this effect.

They might seem a strange spirit animal, but there are more of us akin to ducks than you suppose. In the 1940s and 50s, wall-mounted flying ducks were hugely popular and became a sort of stereotype of lower-middle-class aspiration. They may have been the Marmite of post-war interiors (there's a Kinks song, 'Ducks on the Wall', in which a depressed protagonist bemoans the ones his wife has hung over the fireplace as the antithesis of good taste), but for those who loved them they were comforting and cheery. Their most famous fan, *Coronation Street*'s Hilda Ogden, even credited them with saving her from suicidal thoughts over the years.

Interestingly, the company that made them, Beswick Pottery in Stoke-on-Trent, also produced other bird designs – flying seagulls, pheasants and suchlike – but it was the duck that made it really big.

Ducks have taken on more problematic connotations in recent years. For Millennials and Gen Z, they're not so much aspirational as an avatar for burnout. 'Duck Syndrome' is a term coined by Stanford University to describe students who appear to be gliding through life but in reality are paddling frantically to juggle the impossible demands imposed on their time and attention. It's become a catch-all term for stress, depression and anxiety, and the strange paralysis many of us have felt when faced even with superficially simple tasks, like posting a letter. Having internalised the idea we

A flock of birds flying over Slimbridge Wetland Centre in Gloucestershire.

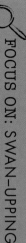

FOCUS ON: SWAN-UPPING

Originally a glorified stocktake of the monarch's poultry larder, the 800-year-old River Thames tradition of swan-upping is now an exercise in conservation. But it also offers a great way to see the aristocrats of the waterfowl world up close.

It's an annual ceremony taking place over five days in summer, in which mute swans are rounded up, weighed, measured, ringed, and then released. A good part of the attraction, aside from the swans, is the pageantry. A flotilla of traditional Thames rowing skiffs, manned by swan-uppers in scarlet rowing shirts and headed by the Queen's Swan Marker, wearing a hat with a white swan's feather, row their way colourfully up the river. 'All up!' they cry as a family of swans and cygnets is spotted, and they cluster around to catch them.

There's not necessarily a 'best place' along the river to watch swan-upping. Most people want to see a swan catch, and that's almost impossible to predict. But you can definitely catch the swan-uppers themselves as they go through the locks, and they're often quite happy to chat.
☛ royal.uk/swans

should be working all the time, we're often just too exhausted to 'adult'.

Ducks on prescription

Curious, then, that ducks don't just describe the condition, but are being used to treat it too, at least in the UK. The Wildfowl & Wetlands Trust's (wwt.org.uk) Blue Prescribing project began at Slimbridge Wetland Centre in Gloucestershire with a pilot scheme for individuals diagnosed with anxiety or depression. Participants took part in a two-hour session per week for six consecutive weeks, in which they went bird-watching, tried bird feeding, had a canoe safari, estuary walk and picnic. The findings showed significant improvements in mental health across a range of indicators, including anxiety, stress and emotional wellbeing. On average, mental wellbeing improved from 'below average' to 'average' by national norms, and participants and healthcare professionals also reported improved physical health and reduced social isolation. It was so successful, similar programmes have been rolled out at WWT Steart Marshes, Somerset and WWT London Wetland Centre.

The results of Blue Prescribing are not unique in finding clear links between birds and wellbeing. In 2017 the University of Exeter, in conjunction with the British Trust for Ornithology and the University of Queensland, surveyed over 270 people from different ages, incomes and ethnicities. It, too, found benefits for mental health in being able to see birds, shrubs and trees around the home, whether people lived in urban or more leafy, suburban neighbourhoods. It also discovered that those who spent less time outdoors than usual in the previous week were more likely to report they were anxious or depressed.

Where to feed them

Convinced? Good, because it's easy to get started. Ducks are pretty ubiquitous on all our inland waterways, whether that's a pond in your local park, the canal that runs behind your bus stop, or the quarry lake at the edge of town. The most common is, of course, the mallard, with as many as 100,000 breeding in the UK, and over 650,000 spending the winter here.

If you want to see a wider range of wildfowl, head over to one of the nine Wildfowl & Wetlands Trust reserves around the UK, of which Slimbridge is the oldest and best known.

WWT has an interesting history. The charity was founded by Peter Scott, the son of Antarctic explorer Captain Scott, who, in his dying letter, urged Peter's

Wigeon in the skies above Buckenham Marshes in Norfolk.

mother to 'make the boy interested in natural history'.

He got what he wanted – and more. Peter became an Olympic sailing medallist and a well-known painter and broadcaster, but conservation was always closest to his heart. As well as WWT, he was the founding chair of WWF and even drew their famous panda logo.

He set up the Wildfowl & Wetlands Trust at Slimbridge in 1946 as a centre for science and conservation. Uniquely at the time, he opened it to the public so that anyone could enjoy getting close to nature. You still can: the centre is open seven days a week, 364 days a year and offers hand-feeding opportunities, bird demonstrations and, frankly, FLAMINGOS.

The colder months are a particularly rewarding time to visit. Up to 30,000 wild ducks, geese, swans and waders

● *Feeding the ducks is a childhood ritual that we'd do well to revive as adults.*

winter at Slimbridge. Look out especially for the enormous flocks of wigeons, teal, lapwings and beautiful Bewick's swans. WWT's Scottish reserve at **Caerlaverock**, Dumfriesshire, meanwhile, has daily 'swan feeds' from October to March where visitors can feast their eyes on wonderful whooper swans while listening to mealtime commentary from the warden.

Wheldrake Ings Nature Reserve (www.ywt.org.uk/nature-reserves/wheldrake-ings-nature-reserve) in Yorkshire is also a solid winter suggestion with plenty of waders and wildfowl, including more whooper swans, widgeons, pintails and teal. Nearby **Fairburn Ings** (www.rspb.org.uk/reserves-and-events/reserves-a-z/fairburn-ings/), run by the RSPB, offers a good chance of sighting the water bird everyone wants a good picture of, the kingfisher. They're a year-round attraction – just keep your eyes and ears peeled for the giveaway flash of blue and 'peep peep'.

In Wales, **Llanbwchllyn Lake**

(www.rwtwales.org/nature-reserves/llanbwchllyn-lake), a nature reserve run by Radnorshire Wildlife Trust, is edged with lush vegetation that gives enticing cover to breeding reed warblers and great crested grebes. It welcomes overwintering wildfowl including goosander, teal, tufted ducks, pochard and goldeneye. Coot and water rail use the reeds as refuge throughout the year. **Portmore Lough** (www.rspb.org.uk/reserves-and-events/reserves-a-z/portmore-lough/) in Co Antrim, Northern Ireland, is another autumn/winter duck spectacle. The reserve is run by the RSPB and sees lots of wildfowl, coot, pochard and tufted duck visitors. Whooper swans and greylag geese arrive from Iceland in October to overwinter at the reserve until April.

How to feed them

Bread is dead. At least, bread-*only* diets are. These days we all need to be much more sophisticated in our waterfowl catering arrangements. The official line from WWT is that bread is okay (wholemeal if possible) as long as it only forms a small part of an otherwise varied menu. This moderation is particularly crucial in spring and summer where young birds could be susceptible to developmental problems if they don't eat a balanced diet.

But there is a more sinister health problem associated with stuffing our lakes, reservoirs and canals with crusts. Too much bread in the water, especially in hot weather, will affect its quality, creating algal problems and the conditions for a disease called botulism to develop, which is a killer for all types of waterfowl. Before a theatre trip in Stratford-upon-Avon one summer evening, I saw a swan die of it in front of my eyes, and it was horrible and still haunts me.

On a more basic level, throwing in too much bread can also lead to overcrowding of bird populations. Not only can this stress ducks and damage their habitats, it also leads to an awful lot of duck mess, which can spell more bad news for water quality.

FOCUS ON: RAFT, BRACE, BROOD OR SKEIN?

If you're going to feed the ducks, you may as well learn the collective noun(s) for them. Getting the correct term, however, all hinges on where they are precisely. On the water? That's a 'raft' you're looking at, probably named for the way they stay packed close to each other for fear of predators.

On the ground, meanwhile, a group of ducks can be a 'waddling' or a 'badelyng' (or 'badling'). If they're babies, go for 'brood'. When in flight, a group of ducks can be called a 'skein', a 'flock' or a 'team'.

Generally speaking, a pair of ducks is called a 'brace' – a term that's often used in hunting to describe other bird and animal pairs ('thirty brace of grouse', for example). Mallards tend to start pairing up in October and November and will usually nest in March.

Interestingly, mallards have their own designations, the most widely used being a 'sord'. But I much prefer 'oiks', the title of a poem about them by former Canal Laureate Jo Bell in her 2015 collection *Kith*, in which they're comically described as thugs and hooligans. The walk may be 'Churchillian', she writes ('chin in and belly first') but there's no hiding the 'stripe of Primark colour on each wing' and all the shouting 'like a bus-stop drunk'.

Only offer food if the birds are taking it and never use old food that is going mouldy. Decomposing bread creates bacteria and tends to attract vermin, especially rats.

Fortunately, there are plenty of good, straightforward alternatives to bread, including sweetcorn, peas, oats and general birdseed. If, like me, you're a chronic waster of bagged lettuce, they'll enjoy the leftovers too, so don't consign it to the bin.

Why to feed them

What my son and I like about feeding ducks is simply that they make us laugh. The waddle, and backchat, the way too many Disney cartoons have set us up for Donald-esque slapstick before we even reach the water's edge. The duckpond we most like visiting is in the centre of a village about 40 minutes' drive from home. We make the effort because the water is so clear we call it the Mallard Maldives, and imagining them all as honeymooning couples is also quite droll. By association, we feel a bit like holidaymakers too, and always leave feeling lighter and happier for it.

Laughing at ducks also makes me better at accepting my own foibles. That

● *Give bread in moderation and only as part of a varied diet.*

walk, those webbed feet, are all quite reasonable in the context of meeting aquatic and terrestrial locomotion halfway. They are the embodiment of a happy medium, of concession. And so when I feel pulled between work and parenting and preparing the dinner and walking the dog and sitting down to write this now, and frustrated that I'm doing the whole lot of it terribly badly, my duck mug consoles me that we're all just shambling along as best we can.

If you do only one thing in this book, make it this. Make it the ducks. I said at the start of this chapter that if the end of the world felt nigh, I would feed the ducks one more time. And this is because ducks, even in our despair, remind us that life probably won't, in fact, end. It goes on, just the same, clamouring to be fed and noticed, full of compromise, and quacks, and oiks, and furious paddling and the grind. But sometimes it looks like gliding. And sometimes it actually is. And have you seen them flying?

Throw something to the ducks – and see if they don't just fling a lifeline back at you.

UNCOMMON AS DUCK

Mallards are probably the limit of most people's fluency with UK ducks, but we actually have 22 regularly occurring species, the majority of which are native. The five below are some of the more striking, and well worth searching out.

Of course, it's all very easy identifying your male ducks in breeding plumage, but when moulting over the summer months they have an altogether different 'eclipse' plumage – a look that's necessarily toned down and more similar in style to waterfowl womenswear. You've been warned.

If you want to get into identifying ducks seriously, I strongly urge you to track down a copy of Peter Scott's *Coloured Key to the Wildfowl of the World*. It contains a coloured illustration of every kind of duck, goose or swan so far known to exist in the world – 245 kinds – to help put a name to the face even without previous 'spotting' experience.

You should also get your head around the two common categories of duck, defined by how they find their food – dabblers or divers. Dabbling ducks stay on the surface and dip their bills into the water. Although they may sometimes 'up-end' to reach deeper, thrusting their heads down, they don't fully submerge.

Diving ducks can actively swim underwater, either chasing prey or taking food from the bottom. Both may also feed on dry land, but dabblers do this much more often. If they're not feeding and you want to tell the difference between the two, look at their back end. A dabbler sits high on the water, with its tail pointing up at an angle. A diver has a lower profile, with the tail close to or even under the water.

MALE

FEMALE

MALE

FEMALE

MANDARIN
These are the real showstoppers of the duck world – but also among the shyest. Originally from eastern Asia, enough mandarins have escaped from exotic wildfowl collections over the years to establish a sizeable breeding population, mainly in southern England. You'll find them on sheltered lakes and lazy rivers with plenty of trees around – and on various pieces of Chinese art, where they represent fidelity and conjugal affection.

GOOSANDER
The beak's the giveaway here – viciously serrated to better catch the fish they prey on. The females are particularly handsome, I think, with their windswept auburn locks. They can be found in the upland rivers of northern England, Scotland and Wales in summer, while in winter they move to lakes, gravel pits and reservoirs.

GOLDENEYE

The male courtship dance in late winter is something to behold – all head-flinging and leg-shaking. The eyes are equally unsettling. Look out for these ducks in the Highlands of Scotland if you're holidaying there this summer. I'm sure they'll have their sneaky yellow gaze fixed on you too.

MALE

FEMALE

TEAL

With an impressive ability to take off almost vertically, these little ducks aren't just a pretty face. If you can look beyond the male's debonair, bright-green eye patch, you may also notice they are Britain's smallest duck.

MALE

FEMALE

TUFTED DUCK

It's the Peaky Blinders undercut that makes this duck easy to recognise. Keeping it classy in black and white (male) and conservative browns (female), the tufted duck is found across the UK at most times of the year, so look out at your local reservoir or lake.

MALE

FEMALE

Main navigation authorities

Broads Authority

Has statutory responsibility for the Norfolk and Suffolk Broads – Britain's largest protected wetland and third largest inland waterway, with the status of a national park. ☛ broads-authority.gov.uk

Canal & River Trust

Looks after over 2,000 miles of canals and rivers, together with reservoirs and a wide range of heritage buildings and structures, in England and Wales. ☛ canalrivertrust.org.uk

Environment Agency

Along with its many other responsibilities, the Environment Agency manages the navigation of the River Thames and the River Medway in the south-east, and many waterways in the Anglian Region. ☛ gov.uk/environment-agency

Lake District National Park Authority

Looks after this unique corner of England, encouraging people to enjoy and understand its beauty and helping those who live and work here. ☛ lakedistrict.gov.uk

National Trust

Not just nice houses, the National Trust also looks after the River Wey and Godalming Navigations and cares for over 20 per cent of the Lake District National Park. ☛ nationaltrust.org.uk

Port of London Authority

PLA's operations cover 95 miles of the River Thames, from Teddington to the North Sea. It works to keep commercial and leisure users safe, protect and enhance the environment, and promote the use of the river for trade and travel. ☛ pla.co.uk

Scottish Canals

Cares for 137 miles of waterway network in total, including five canals, 17 reservoirs and the navigation rights to four lochs, including Loch Ness. ☛ scottishcanals.co.uk

Waterways Ireland

Responsible for the management, maintenance, development, and restoration of inland navigable waterways in Ireland and Northern Ireland. ☛ waterwaysireland.org

Conservation and campaigning

Inland Waterways Association

Formed in 1946 to campaign for the conservation, use, maintenance, restoration and sensitive development of British canals and river navigations. ☛ waterways.org.uk

River Thames Society

A membership organisation dedicated to conserving the Thames for future generations and representing all river users, whether they be fishermen, walkers, boatowners or just interested in its very rich history, traditions, flora and fauna. ☛ riverthamessociety.org.uk

Thames21

Working with communities across Greater London to improve its rivers, canals, ponds and lakes for people and wildlife. ☛ thames21.org.uk

The Rivers Trust

An environmental charity and an umbrella organisation for 60 member trusts concerned with rivers in England, Wales, Northern Ireland and Ireland. ☛ theriverstrust.org

The Royal Lifesaving Society UK
Founded in 1891 with the aim of safeguarding lives in, on and near water. It trains over 93 per cent of all pool and beach lifeguards throughout the UK and Ireland. 🖝 rlss.org.uk

Access

Right to Roam
Campaigning to extend the Countryside & Rights of Way (CRoW) Act in England so that millions more people can have easy access to open space, including on rivers and lakes.
🖝 righttoroam.org.uk

Scottish Outdoor Access Code
Detailed information on your rights and responsibilities in the Scottish outdoors, including in or along its waterways.
🖝 www.outdooraccess-scotland.scot/

Boating and watersports

Beyond Swim
Launched in 2021, Beyond Swim was created by Triathlon England (and is supported by Swim England and Royal Lifesaving Society) to provide venue accreditation and give open water swimmers of all abilities enjoyable and consistent experiences.
🖝 beyondswim.org

British Canoeing
National governing body for canoeing in the UK, established in 1936 as the British Canoe Union.
🖝 britishcanoeing.org.uk

British Rowing
National governing body for the sport of rowing.
🖝 britishrowing.org

British Stand Up Paddle Association
Leading the development of the sport through training/coaching schemes for UK SUP schools, plus competitive and fun events. 🖝 www.bsupa.org.uk/

British Swimming
The national governing body of swimming, including open water swimming, in Great Britain.
🖝 britishswimming.org

Canoe Association of Northern Ireland
Governing body for canoeing and kayaking in Northern Ireland.
🖝 cani.org.uk

Canoe Wales
National governing body for paddlesport in Wales. 🖝 canoewales.com

Go Paddling
Great resource for recreational paddlers, whether you're brand new to the sport or a confident paddler looking to take on new adventures on the water.
🖝 gopaddling.info

On the Water
The brainchild of trade association British Marine, this useful website is designed to connect people with fully checked-out boating and watersports providers. Whether you want to paddleboard, kayak, hire a boat or just want to see what's on offer in an area, search by postcode, book directly with a provider and that's it, you're on the water.
🖝 onthewater.co.uk

Outdoor Swimmer
Monthly magazine for outdoor swimmers 'to provide inspiration for people who swim outdoors and to help readers live healthier and happier lives through outdoor swimming'.
🖝 outdoorswimmer.com

Rowing Ireland
Cross-border national governing body for rowing in Ireland.
🖝 rowingireland.ie

Royal Yachting Association
The national governing body for sailing, dinghy sailing, yacht and motor cruising, sail racing, RIBs and sportsboats, windsurfing and personal watercraft

and a leading representative for inland waterways cruising.
☞ rya.org.uk

Scottish Canoe Association
National governing body for canoeing in Scotland. ☞ canoescotland.org

Swim Ireland
The national governing body for swimming, including open water swimming, in Ireland and Northern Ireland. ☞ swimireland.ie

The Outdoor Swimming Society
The OSS encourages people to rediscover the joys of swimming in open, wild water – whether that be rivers, lakes, lochs, tarns, ponds or seas – and provides information about safety and access.
☞ outdoorswimmingsociety.com

Waterways World
Britain's best-selling canal and river magazine since 1972, with advice, ideas, inspirational features and regular podcasts. ☞ waterwaysworld.com

Walking, running and cycling

Cycle.Travel
Free, easy-to-use cycle route planner plus detailed guides to classic routes.
☞ cycle.travel

Ramblers
Britain's leading walking charity, with around 100,000 members and a network of volunteers who maintain and protect the path network.
☞ ramblers.org.uk

Sustrans
Walking, wheeling and cycling charity, and the custodian of the National Cycle Network. ☞ sustrans.org.uk

The Outdoor Guide
Contains a good selection of Julia Bradbury's canal walks for the seasoned stomper.
☞ theoutdoorguide.co.uk

Trail Running Association
Promotes and encourages participation in trail running throughout the UK and provides guidance and facilities for organisers of trail races.
☞ tra-uk.org

Fishing

Angling Trust
Promotes anglers' rights, fish conservation, preservation of habitat, and fish and angler welfare.
☞ anglingtrust.net

Holidays and camping

Camping and Caravanning Club
Founded in 1901, the club represents over half a million members and is involved with all aspects of camping in the UK.
☞ campingandcaravanningclub.co.uk

CanalAbility
Charity, with over 25 years of experience, dedicated to providing affordable canal boat holidays and day trips for people with disabilities, their families, friends and other disability charities and community groups.
☞ canalability.org.uk

Caravan and Motorhome Club
Membership organisation representing caravan and motorhome users in the UK, formerly The Caravan Club.
☞ caravanclub.co.uk

Drifters

A consortium of privately owned self-drive hire-boat companies set up to promote enjoyment of canal holidays and operating from 47 sites spread throughout the canals of England, Wales and Scotland, as well as sites on the Fens and River Thames.

☛ drifters.co.uk

Living afloat

National Bargee Travellers Association

Represents the interests of itinerant liveaboard boaters.

☛ bargee-traveller.org.uk

Residential Boat Owners' Association

Welcomes members who live, aspire to or support life afloat. ☛ rboa.org.uk

STUDY AND ARTICLE REFERENCES

(p6) Canal & River Trust, 'Waterways & Wellbeing' report, 2017
☛ canalrivertrust.org.uk/refresh/media/thumbnail/33802-canal-and-river-trust-outcomes-report-waterways-and-wellbeing-full-report.pdf

(p7) After the first lockdown, British Canoeing reported an exponential growth in membership, welcoming over 25,000 new paddlers to its community.
☛ www.britishcanoeing.org.uk/news/2020/british-canoeing-report-record-growth-in-membership-figures

(p7) The Canal & River Trust also noted a huge spike in towpath use, particularly along urban navigations.
☛ https://canalrivertrust.org.uk/news-and-views/news/towpaths-to-remain-open-during-national-restrictions

(p10) Environment Agency Water Framework Directive Classification Status data:
☛ deframedia.blog.gov.uk/2020/09/18/latest-water-classifications-results-published/

(p10) In 2021, environmental charity Thames21 released a laser scan showing the extent that a mound of them in the riverbed in west London had grown:
☛ www.thames21.org.uk/2021/11/laser-scans-show-devastating-impact-of-wet-wipes-on-the-thames/

(p11) The Canal & River Trust has a Plastics Challenge in which you pledge to pick up just one piece of plastic.
☛ canalrivertrust.org.uk/news-and-views/features/plastic-and-litter-in-our-canals

(p11) Non-native Species Secretariat report on freshwater species:
☛ www.nonnativespecies.org/what-can-i-do/check-clean-dry/

(p14) The woman grieving her son, *Guardian*, March 2020
☛ https://amp.theguardian.com/society/2021/mar/20/my-son-felix-was-20-when-he-died-better-awareness-of-epilepsy-might-have-saved-him

(p29) Back in 2017, Scottish Canals launched a so-called Selfie Trail to get more families out exploring the Forth & Clyde Canal between the Falkirk Wheel and the Kelpies
☛ www.scottishcanals.co.uk/news/public-invited-take-journey-selfie-discovery-along-forth-clyde-canal/

(p40) My first assignment on joining the editorial team of *Waterways World*, a monthly canal magazine, was to interview an elderly couple who had been hiring boats every year for half a century
'A Half Century of Hiring', *Waterways World*, April 2015

(p78) In May 2021 the Canal & River Trust incorporated paddleboarding into an innovative social prescribing project on the Nottingham & Beeston Canal
☛ canalrivertrust.org.uk/news-and-views/news/social-prescribing-project-receives-gbp50000

☛ canalrivertrust.org.uk/about-us/where-we-work/east-midlands/social-prescribing-in-nottingham

(p82) 2020 Bridgewater Canal survey into the health and wellbeing benefits of the canal during Covid-19 lockdowns
☛ peellandp.co.uk/news-and-views/news/bridgewater-canal-helps-improve-people-s-mental-health-and-wellbeing-during-covid-19-lockdowns/

(p84) *Gaudy Night* by Dorothy L Sayers (Hodder & Stoughton), reproduced by permission of David Higham Associates

(p86) 'Worth a Punt', *Thames Guardian*, Autumn 2019

(p92) Joint study by the University of California and Trinity College, Dublin that focused on the emotional benefits of so-called 'awe walks' in older adults
☛ www.ucsf.edu/news/2020/09/418551/awe-walks-boost-emotional-well-being

(p100) Historic England's Heritage and Society report in 2019
☛ historicengland.org.uk/content/heritage-counts/pub/2019/heritage-and-society-2019/

(p108) Nowka Bais quote from *Waterways World*
'The BAME Game', *Waterways World*, September 2020

(p122) In 2019, scientists from the Department of Neuroscience at the University of Geneva studied this more closely on a group of 18 healthy young volunteers
☛ www.cell.com/current-biology/pdf/S0960-9822(18)31662-2.pdf

(p134) 'Commuting: The stress that doesn't pay' ran the headline of a *Psychology Today* article in 2015
☛ www.psychologytoday.com/gb/blog/urban-survival/201501/commuting-the-stress-doesnt-pay

(p138) Glasgow City Council is reportedly looking at the feasibility of launching commuter boat travel on the Forth & Clyde Canal with a water bus
☛ www.glasgowtimes.co.uk/news/19572098.glasgow-water-bus-m8-garden-among-projects-considered-councillors/

(p148) IWA volunteer feature in *Waterways World*
'The Offside Rule', *Waterways World*, May 2020

(p148) CRT published a report revealing the economic and social value of volunteering to the organisation, to those who volunteer and to wider society, 2021
☛ canalrivertrust.org.uk/refresh/media/original/45095-the-value-of-volunteering-2021.pdf

(p156) Canal & River Trust's Annual Lockage Report 2021
☛ canalrivertrust.org.uk/refresh/media/original/45293-annual-lockage-report-2021.pdf

(p157) Two testimonials of volunteers from an article, 'Restoration Woman', IWA *Waterways*, Spring 2021

(p162) 1896, Arthur Conan Doyle was asked to publicly endorse this new obsession for *Scientific American*
☛ *Scientific American*, New York, January 18, 1896, Vol. LXXIV, NO. 3

(p177) Hornby's chief executive Lyndon Davies probably got near the nub of it when commenting on his own company's pandemic boom to the *Guardian* in 2020
☛ www.theguardian.com/lifeandstyle/2020/oct/25/we-are-railing-britain-embraces-the-joys-of-the-humble-train-set

(p190) Canal & River Trust figures show that from 2012 to 2019, boat numbers in London grew by 84 per cent, while continuously cruising boats (those without a fixed mooring) soared by 246 per cent.
☛ canalrivertrust.org.uk/news-and-views/news/improvements-to-london-canals-announced-as-boat-numbers-soar

(p190) Strutt & Parker, who surveyed 2,000 people as part of their 2018 Waterside Survey
☛ www.struttandparker.com/about-strutt-parker/corporate-news/young-adults-driving-the-demand-for-waterside-living

(p191) Claudia Jessie interview in *Waterways World*
'The Boating Bridgerton', *Waterways World*, May 2021

(p191) Nicola Thorp interview in *Waterways World*
'Soap and Water', *Waterways World*, August 2020

(p196) The study, published in the March 2022 issue of the *International Journal of Hygiene and Environmental Health*, found people living in deprived areas near the now restored Forth & Clyde Canal had a 15 per cent lower risk of cardiovascular disease, a stroke or hypertension. It also correlated with a 12 per cent lower risk of diabetes and 10 per cent reduction in obesity.
☛ www.gcu.ac.uk/theuniversity/universitynews/2022-livingnearacanalcutschronicdisease/

(p206) The Wildfowl & Wetlands Trust's (wwt.org.uk) Blue Prescribing project began at Slimbridge Wetland Centre in Gloucestershire with a pilot scheme for individuals diagnosed with anxiety or depression
☛ www.mdpi.com/1660-4601/16/22/4413

(p206) In 2017 the University of Exeter, in conjunction with the British Trust for Ornithology and the University of Queensland, surveyed over 270 people from different ages ☛ www.exeter.ac.uk/news/featurednews/title_571299_en.html

BIBLIOGRAPHY/FURTHER READING

Helen Babbs, *Adrift: A Secret Life of London's Waterways* (Icon Books, 2016)

Jo Bell, *Kith* (Nine Arches Press, 2015)

RD Blackmore, *Lorna Doone* (Wordsworth, 1993)

William Bliss, *The Heart of England by Waterway* (London: H.F. & G. Witherby, 1933)

Lizzie Carr, *Paddling Britain: 50 Best Places to Explore by SUP, Kayak & Canoe* (Bradt Travel Guides, 2018)

Danie Couchman, *Afloat: A Memoir* (Quadrille, 2019)

Rachel Cullen, *Running For My Life: How I Built a Better Me One Step at a Time* (Blink Publishing, 2018)

Roger Deakin, *Waterlog* (Vintage, 2000)

Lori de Mori and Laura Jackson, *Towpath: Recipes & Stories* (Chelsea Green Publishing, 2020)

Julian Dutton, *Water Gypsies: A History of Life on Britain's Rivers and Canals* (The History Press, 2021)

David Fathers, *London's Hidden Rivers: A Walker's Guide to the Subterranean Waterways of London* (Frances Lincoln, 2017)

Alys Fowler, *Hidden Nature: A Voyage of Discovery* (Hodder, 2018)

Tristan Gooley, *How to Read Water: Clues & Patterns from Puddles to the Sea* (Sceptre, 2017)

Kenneth Grahame, *The Wind in the Willows* (Penguin Classics, 2005)

Simon Griffiths, *Swim Wild and Free: A Practical Guide to Swimming Outdoors 365 Days a Year* (Bloomsbury Sport, 2022)

Isabel Hardman, *The Natural Health Service: How Nature Can Mend Your Mind* (Atlantic Books, 2021)

Jerome K Jerome, *Three Men in a Boat* (Penguin Classics, 1999)

Lucy Jones, *Losing Eden: Why Our Minds Need the Wild* (Penguin, 2021)

Tony Jones, *The Liveaboard Guide: Living Afloat on the Inland Waterways* 2nd edition (Adlard Coles, 2019)

Dr Catherine Kelly, *Blue Spaces: How & Why Water Can Make You Feel Better* (Welbeck Balance, 2021)

William Manners, *Revolution: How the Bicycle Reinvented Modern Britain* (Duckworth, 2019)

Di Murrell, *A Foodie Afloat* (Matador, 2021)

Stephen Neale, *Camping by the Waterside: The Best Campsites by Water in Britain and Ireland*, 2nd edition (Adlard Coles, 2017)

Wallace J Nichols, *Blue Mind: How Water Makes You Happier, More Connected and Better at What You Do* (Abacus, 2018)

Dave Price, *The Paddleboard Bible: The Complete Guide to Stand-up Paddleboarding* (Adlard Coles, 2021)

Dorothy L Sayers, *Gaudy Night* (Hodder & Stoughton, 2016)

Peter Scott, *Peter Scott's Coloured Key to the Wildfowl of the World* (The Wildfowl & Wetlands Trust, 2006)

RL Stevenson, *An Inland Voyage*

Jasper Winn, *Water Ways: A Thousand Miles Along Britain's Canals* (Profile, 2020)

John Wright, *Hedgerow* (River Cottage Handbook, No.7) (Bloomsbury, 2010)

Chris Yates, *The Lost Diary: A Summer Fishing in Pursuit of Golden Scales* (Unbound, 2013)

Anne Young, *Paint Roses and Castles: Traditional Narrow Boat Painting for Homes and Boats* (David & Charles, 1992)

LOCATIONS INDEX

GENERAL INDEX

PICTURE CREDITS

(Top/middle/bottom = **T/M/B**, Left/Right = **L/R**)

p1 © Maskot, Getty Images; **p2–3** © Davina/ Image Bliss Photography; **p4–5** © Agustin Oshee/ EyeEm, Getty Images; **p6** © Pixdeluxe, Getty Images; **p8–9** © Paulo Sousa/EyeEm, Getty Images; **p10** © Tim Robberts, Getty Images; **p12–3** © Westend61, Getty Images; **p14–5** and **p16–7** © Luis Alvarez, Getty Images; **p18** © K Neville, Getty Images; **p19** © Loop Images, Getty Images; **p20T** © SOPA Images, Getty Images; **p20B** R Boed, via Wikimedia Commons; **p21** © Thames Lido; **p22–3** © Ruth Slater; **p24–5** © Jo Hale, Getty Images; **p26–7** © Tim Heaton (cc-by-sa/2.0), geograph.org; **p28** © S Turner, Getty Images; **p30** © Loop Images, Getty Images; **p31** © Shomos Udon, Getty Images; **p32** © Education Images, Getty Images; **p33** © Des Green, Getty Images; **p35** © Ross Woodhall, Getty Images; **p37** © Rachel Cullen; **p38–9** © blue sky in my pocket, Getty Images; **p40** Jonathan Blackham, Getty Images; **p41** © CanalAbility; **p42** © Education Images, Getty Images; **p43** © Robert Bray, Getty Images; **p44** © blue sky in my pocket, Getty Images; **p45** © Johner Images, Getty Images; **p46–7** © Education Images, Getty Images; **p48T** © Andrew Denny; **p48B** © David Hawgood, Creative Commons, geograph.org.uk; **p49** © Sarah Henshaw; **p50–1** © David Suchet; **p52–3** © RunPhoto, Getty Images; **p55** © jeffbergen, Getty Images; **p56** © georgeclerk, Getty Images; **p58** © Tackling Minds; **p59–60** © Leonie Paterson; **p62** © Leon Neale, Getty Images; **p63** © Alexander Scharafin, Getty Images; **p64–5** © zeljkosantrac, Getty Images; **p66–7** © Sarah Henshaw; **p68T** © SOPA Images, Getty Images; **p68B** © Education Images, Getty Images; **p70** © Sam Mellish, Getty Images; **p73** © Sally Anscombe, Getty Images; **p74** © Helen Tidy; **p76–7** © Sam Mellish, Getty Images; **p78T** and **p78M** © Richard Baker, Getty Images; **p79** © Leon Neal, Getty Images; **p81** © Richard Drury, Getty Images; **p82T** © TravellingLight, Getty Images; **p82M** © Imre Cikajlo, Getty Images; **p82B** © ClickAndPray Photography, Getty Images; **p83** © Sophy Aykroyd; **p84–5** © Loop Images, Getty Images; **p86** © Hutton Archive, Getty Images; **p87** © Paul Popper/Popperfoto, Getty Images; **p88** © Heritage Images, Getty Images; **p89** © Patrick Aventurier, Getty Images; **p90–1** © Mike Kemp, Getty Images; **p92** © Rosser1954, Wikimedia Commons; **p93T** © Ian Pudsey, Wikimedia Commons; **p93B** © David Dixon, Wikimedia Commons; **p94ML** © Brenda Kean, Getty Images; **p94MR** © Neil Forsyth, Wikimedia Commons; **p94B** © Rev Dave, Wikimedia Commons; **p95T** © Alasdair James, Getty Images; **p95B** © Alistair Dick, Getty Images; **p96** and **p97** © MyLoupe, Getty Images; **p98T** © Education Images, Getty Images; **p98ML**, **p98M** and **p98MR** © Sarah Henshaw; **p98B** © Caitlin Mogridge, Getty Images; **p101** © View Pictures, Getty Images; **p103** © Bethany Clarke, Getty Images; **p104–5** © Planet One Images, Getty Images; **p107T** and **p107B** © SolStock, Getty Images; **p108T** © Anadolu Agency, Getty Images; **p108B** © Alex Broadway, Getty Images; **p109T** © Dan Kitwood, Getty Images; **p109B** © Nowka Bais CIC; **p110** © Gerard Wilcox; **p111** © Plume Creative, Getty Images; **p112** © MyLoupe, Getty Images; **p113** © Loop Images, Getty Images; **p114** © Nick Daly, Getty Images; **p116L** © Michael Robert, Getty Images; **p116R** © Barrington Coombs, Getty Images; **p117** and **p119** © Colin McPherson, Getty Images; **p120–1** © Platoo fotography, Getty Images; **p122** © Fabrice LEROUGE, Getty Images; **p123** © Erin J Short; **p124–5** © Rich Jones Photography, Getty Images; **p126–7** © Maskot, Getty Images; **p128** © Duncan Fawkes, Getty Images; **p129T** © Andrea Pistolesi, Getty Images; **p129B** © Davina/ Image Bliss Photography; **p131** © Jasper Winn; **p132–3** © oversnap, Getty Images; **p134–5** © Peter Trimming, Wikimedia Commons; **p136** and **p137** © Chris Smith; **p138T** © vandervelden, Getty Images; **p138B** © P A Thompson, Getty Images; **p139** © Duncan1890, Getty Images; **p140** © Terje Lein-Mathisen, Getty Images; **p141** © Julian Kennard; **p142T** © Image by Nonac_Digi for the Green Man, Getty Images; **p142B** © Westend61, Getty Images; **p143** © Mattbuck, Wikimedia Commons; **p144–5** © Universal Images Group, Getty Images; **p146–7** © Photo_Concepts, Getty Images; **p149** © Stockbyte, Getty Images, **p150** © Nattapong Wongloungud / EyeEm, Getty Images; **p151** © mladenbalinovac, Getty Images; **p152** © Rosie Landers; **p153T** and **p153L** © Sarah Henshaw; **p153R** © Maskot, Getty Images; **p154** © Canal & River Trust; **p155T** © Sawitree Pamee / EyeEm, Getty Images; **p155B** © Peter Muller, Getty Images; **p156** © Andrew Denny; **p157** © IWA/WRG; **p159T** © Mike Gilham; **p159B** © Steve Ashley; **p160–1** © Milo Zanecchia/ Ascent Xmedia, Getty Images; **p163** © Roy James Shakespeare, Getty Images; **p164** © Michael Herrfernan, Getty Images; **p165** © Erik Isakson, Getty Images;

223

p166 Sustrans, Wikimedia Commons; **p167** © Friends of the Montgomery Canal; **p169** © Marine Dimeck, Getty Images; **p171** © Richard Fairhurst; **p172** © Andrea Pucci, Getty Images; **p173** © Peter Sandground, Scottish Canals; **p174–5** © Oliver Rossi, Getty Images; **p176** © CreativeDJ, Getty Images; **p177** © SolStock, Getty Images; **p178** © Slavica, Getty Images; **p179** © Lucy Lambriex, Getty Images; **p180** © Canal & River Trust; **p181** © Education Images, Getty Images; **p182** © Holly Robbins; **p184–5** © Donald Iain Smith, Getty Images; **p186–7** © DGLimages, Getty Images; **p188–9** © Hannah Bodsworth; **p190** © Roy James Shakespeare, Getty Images; **p191** and **p192** © Johnny Greig, Getty Images; **p194** © Igor Emmerich, Getty Images; **p195** © Roy James Shakespeare, Getty Images; **p196–7** © Joe Daniel Price, Getty Images; **p199** © Anthony Wigley; **p200–1** © Hannah Bodsworth; **p202–3** © Sally Anscombe, Getty Images; **p204–5** © N-Photo Magazine, Getty Images; **p205R** © WPA Pool, Getty Images; **p206** © Education Images, Getty Images; **p207** © Sarah Henshaw; **p209** © ZenShui/Yves Regaldi, Getty Images.

ACKNOWLEDGEMENTS

This book would not have been possible without my six years on the editorial team at *Waterways World* magazine. Many of the chapters (especially those on hire-boating, days out, volunteering and living afloat) are scaffolded by the people I interviewed in that time and the breadth of features I was encouraged to write. I am grateful for all I learned, and for the generosity, wisdom and friendship of my colleagues there, especially Peter Johns (publisher), Amelia Hamson, Andrew Denny and its editor, Bobby Cowling.

Thank you to all the people who shared their waterways stories and wealth of experience with me, including those who aren't mentioned specifically in the text: Gary O'Daly, Suzanne Rowcliffe, Roger Ireland, Ruth Slater, Rachel Cullen, David Suchet, David Lyons, Leonie Paterson, Helen Tidy, Gael Robertson, Chris Smith, Gerard Wilcox, Hannah Bodsworth, Jasper Winn, Julian Kennard, Mike Gilham, Richard Fairhurst, Rosie Landers, Sophy Ackroyd and Tony Jones.

Special mention also to Peter Finch of the River Thames Society, who was full of help, as he always is, and to the team at Bloomsbury for guiding me from proposal to publication, especially Clara Jump.

My parents always made time for us to enjoy water as children – on beaches, in pools, by canals and in the garden – and I am endlessly grateful. They gave me the time, too, to finish writing this. Thank you.

This book is dedicated to the memory of Ashling Murphy, whose death made headlines as I was writing the running chapter. Jogging alongside the water can be one of life's great pleasures. Let's, all of us, keep the towpaths busy, and in that way safer, for people who want to use them without fear.

Finally, to Stu and Seth, 'SS', the good ship, who I have the privilege to be carried on every day. With all my love.